16

Talcott Parsons

An Introduction

Sandro Segre

UNIVERSITY PRESS OF AMERICA,® INC.

Lanham • Boulder • New York • Toronto • Plymouth, UK

Library of Congress Control Number: 2011928826
ISBN: 978-0-7618-5586-6 (clothbound : alk. paper)
ISBN: 978-0-7618-5587-3 (paperback : alk. paper)
eISBN: 978-0-7618-5588-0

Contents

Introduction

Talcott Parsons (1902–1979), one of the most influential and well-known sociologists of the twentieth century, is the author of an enormous body of work which has aroused disputes and been subject to divergent interpretations. After some discussion of the conceptual aspect of his thought, we shall follow the conventional division of his work into different periods (Alexander 1983: 46–48, 73–77, 119–120; Hamilton 1989; see also Gerhardt 2002: 58). In support of the decision to adhere to this division, we refer to the differences emerging in epistemological assumptions, theoretical references, and the conceptual patterns in his thought, in particular, the concepts of action and voluntarism, as they are manifest in each period. The thesis of diversity, though adopted by several of his interpreters, has however been supported in different ways and with different arguments (see, for instance, Scott 1963 and Alexander's critical remarks in this connection, 1983, 34, 334–335). Instead of emphasizing diversity in the development of his work, some commentators prefer to focus on continuity. In their opinion, over the various decades of his career, there was a progressive improvement in the theoretical analysis of single conceptual nucleus of insights (Muench 1982).

We will here limit ourselves to arguing that different themes prevailed during Parsons' various periods of productivity. A first period in the 1930s, was characterized by an in-depth study of some European authors—Durkheim, Pareto and Weber. Parsons greatly contributed to their public recognition in the United States through the release of "The Structure of Social Action" (1937). Several minor texts both anticipate and accompany this major work (Camic 1991, lxv-lxviii). During the central period (up till the early 1960s), Parsons developed some new theories by drawing on the complex conceptual apparatus he had created. In the final period of his life, from about the mid-1960s to his death (1979), Parsons focused primarily on the theme of social change, for which he developed an evolutionary explanation.

The first, introductory section of this book is devoted to outlining Parsons' conceptual apparatus; subsequently, we consider the various periods of his development. Each will therefore be discussed separately. The second section of our discussion reveals a continuous progression of concepts and explanatory patterns on Parsons' part. These are often described as theories. Also, several of Parsons' studies focused on specific themes, e.g., the concepts of power and influence, ethnic groups, their nature and social stratification, and also on studies in which those concepts and patterns have been applied. These studies were carried out by others. Parsons referred to them for the purpose of undergirding his theoretical statements with empirical references (Lidz 2000: 420). They focused on democracy, political power, medical profession and health sociology, the education system in Germany and in the United States, family, youth culture, deviance and secularization.

Finally, this book also provides some information about the wide and varied reception of his work. It distinguishes between works published during Parsons' life (to which he could reply) (Parsons 1961a) and those published after his death, and also between general introductions to his work and particular periods.

Chapter One

The Conceptual Apparatus

In what follows, we report the meanings, as Parsons indicated them, of some concepts which are either frequent or recurrent in his production. They will subsequently be explained in greater detail. Their definitions have been directly drawn from his writings (Parsons 1934; 1949: 43–51, 74–77, 731–748; 1951: 4–5, 11–12, 19–22, 25–36, 48–49, 51–55, 58–67, 79–88, 133–136, 403–405, 480–496, 512–515, 537–541; 1961a; 1961b: 33–49; 1964a: 123–125; 1964b; 1966: 5–29; 1970; 1977; 1978; 2007; Parsons, Bales, Shils 1953: 4–10, 85–109, 163–190; Parsons, Shils 2001; Parsons, Smelser 1957: 101–103). On certain specific points, as well as for interpretations and analyses of these texts, reference will also be made to additional sources. However, in this chapter, we shall not consider the shifts in meaning that these concepts may have undergone over time or their use in different periods (Johnson 1975: 3–4, 26). Some indications of this will be provided in the next chapters. At present we wish to focus exclusively on the stable elements of his conceptual apparatus.

For Parsons, *Theory* is understood as a system of laws grounded on empirical generalizations. *Action* indicates a relation with an external object, which is justified and significant for an actor. An *actor* is intended both as a behavioral system, and as a personality system. In the second sense, an actor is a subject provided with knowledge which he or she uses to consciously orient his or her action in roles he or she plays and in the communities of which he or she is a member. A theory of action aims at identifying, through an analytical abstraction process, the conceptual elements which constitute an action. *Unit acts,* the acts forming the unit of analysis, are those analytical elements which are considered useful in shedding light on the elementary components of each action and on the relations among actions within an "action scheme" or an "action system." The conceptual elements of a theory of action, being of

1

an analytical nature, cannot be found in empirical reality. This pattern acts as a "frame of reference," in the sense that it provides the conceptual apparatus through which any empirically existing action system can be analyzed.

The formulation of a "general theory of action" requires a preliminary formulation of general propositions including interconnected and clearly defined concepts, but these concepts do not form a logical-deductive system. Even though knowledge that allows for the formulation of a "general theory"—in the sense of a system of empirical generalizations is lacking, it is still possible to formulate "paradigms," that is to say, criteria, standards, or "canons," through which one can understand the relations existing among the fundamental variables of a system. Analytically considered, an action is any behavior that can be examined in its constitutive elements as follows: a behavior assumes there is an actor; it is oriented to a future condition anticipated by the actor; it takes place in a situation which an actor does not fully control, one that differs from what he or she anticipated; it involves being able to distinguish the characteristics of an object or of a category of objects (possibly also of another individual) and to attribute importance to it; it is regulated by norms, therefore the actor considers it desirable and compulsory; it requires a motivation or an effort by one or more actors. Parsons borrows a term from psychoanalysis to describe the attribution of importance and the attachment to an object, and particularly to another actor: *cathexis.*

An "actor," be it an individual or a collectivity, can either orient himself or herself to obtaining from the outer world a maximum amount of benefits at a minimum cost, or, he or she can orient himself or herself to a situation which he or she defines as relevant, one that conforms to his or her own interests. An action is "instrumental" when the actor carries it out in order to obtain a future reward, one which would not be obtained without his or her intervention. By contrast, an action is "expressive" when it is oriented to the purpose of organizing the reward flow and preventing deprivation of the desired object. A situation can be diverse in nature, depending on the object to which it is oriented: it can be social (one or more actors are the object of the orientation), cultural (ideas, beliefs, rules, values), or physical. Orienting oneself to a situation implies that the actor has a motivation to address himself or herself to a particular object. This involves an effort on his part, and he does not do it based exclusively on a cost-benefit evaluation, but rather because he is driven to act on impulse and his motivations ("need dispositions") are constantly organized by certain cognitive and evaluative elements. These, in turn, make it possible for him or her not to orient his or her action only to the present situation.

A "system" is a stable set of interdependent phenomena, provided with analytically-established boundaries, which relates to an ever-changing external environment. A "social system" is a system of social interactions between reciprocally oriented actors. It consists of roles, collectivities, norms and values. The social system forms a system of societies, each characterized by relative autonomy, by its own territorial organization, and by its own sense of identity. In a social system, actors relate to one another by jointly orienting themselves to a situation through a language or other shared symbols. A social system comprises several subsystems or collectivities, all of which are functionally differentiated, interdependent and intertwined. Analysis of such a systems focuses on the conditions in which interactions occur within particular collectivities.

A "cultural system," by contrast, is defined as an orderly pattern of meanings. It is socially produced and consists of relatively stable symbolic systems which are passed on through values, norms, beliefs and organized knowledge. A society is a particular collectivity formed by a set of organized relations resulting from interactions between individuals; it is self-sufficient in relation to its environment. Self-sufficiency, in this sense, means that: a) a society is not a subsystem of a more generalized system; b) interchanges with the environment are stable and subject to its control. In this way, it is possible to meet the necessary condition that allows a society, and a social system in general, to face the inconveniences that come from the external environment. System differentiation into functionally specialized parts is another necessary condition.

Finally, a "personality system" is the action system of a single actor. Since it is a system, the actor's actions are connected with each other, compatible and integrated. Their organization results from the existence of the actor's needs as they have stabilized, i.e. they have solidified into the actor's own attitudes or need dispositions as concerns his or her actions towards other objects, and particularly other human beings. The term "need dispositions" in fact defines needs that have become stable dispositions of the actor's personality. This term refers to the fact that values and roles, i.e. elements external to the actor, which are learned by him or her, can integrate, coordinate and change the fulfillment of his or her needs. Examples of need dispositions, according to Parsons, are not only one's need to be esteemed and obtain approval, responses and love, but also values and roles themselves. "Roles," in fact, correspond to an individual's need to stabilize and socially integrate the merely individual needs of the personality system (see Baldwin 1961: 158–162; Joas, Knoebl 2009: 60–67; Prandini 1998: 11–12, 33–34 and Note No. 8).

Functions are sets of conditions both within and outside the system which set limits on the system variations that are compatible with its integrity and effectiveness. They concern relations based on mutual adaptation or integration among the elements of the social system, and conversely, social system's adaptation to its various environments. Functions therefore also relate to the stability or instability of the social system, its survival and ability to persist in relation to the environments in which it is included. They point out the consequences of processes carried out by actors and communities in the social structure, and are distinguished into instrumental and expressive functions. Instrumental functions involve a systemic orientation to the attainment of some purpose. Their prevalence in the system therefore makes it necessary to consider them from an instrumental point of view. Expressive functions, by contrast, involve a systemic *cathectic* orientation, in virtue of which shared feelings of attachment and loyalty to a collectivity are institutionalized among the actors.

A social role is a stable interaction. It is ruled by norms which establish the rights and the obligations of the members of a collectivity. Roles are the constitutive units of the social system. They are functionally differentiated from one another. A functional analysis focuses both on social structures and on processes. The term *social structure* designates stable social interaction systems. The stability or equilibrium of these systems depends on the reciprocal orientation and consistency of the interests of actors as they are placed within in a system of differentiated roles. System stability does not necessarily imply immobility, because a system subject to an orderly change is in a state of equilibrium as is a static one. A condition of *strain* may be the consequence of an actor's defective integration into an interaction system. Internal conflicts in the actor's personality can be the result of this strain, as can frustrations of his expectations that others reciprocate his orientation; resentment and hostility towards others are also possible consequences. Defective integration may, in turn, be the result of conflicts, and in general, of ineffective integration into the roles which make up the social system (Johnson 1975: 36–40). System stability can be empirically identified; it can also be assumed when certain circumstances are considered relevant to particular investigations (Parsons 1951: 36, 490–492; see also Devereux 1961: 51–52, 59–60). *Process* indicates the elements of a system that are important from a theoretical point of view. These elements change over the time interval that is considered significant for such investigation.

A *collectivity* is a social system characterized by both the fact that some purpose is shared by several actors who are all oriented toward certain institutionalized values; it can also be a single interaction system, the boundaries of which are set by the roles that constitute it. Norms can be either specific for each particular role or function, or they can be shared by the participants in a social system, regardless of the peculiar roles they play. In the second case, they are designated as values. Values indicate an orientation, considered desirable, of one or more actors to an object or a class of objects in a given situation. Values, jointly considered, are a constitutive element of the social system. They, in turn, form a system, and are necessary to bring about the integration of the social system. A social system is integrated when its constitutive roles, i.e., the norms that govern role behaviors, are consistent and coordinated. The term *institution* defines the general conditions of stability of a social system. These result from the need to meet its functional prerequisites. In other words, an institution can be understood as a set of rules, norms and principles which establish the performances and determine the sanctions that are functionally necessary to the system.

This involves regulating social relations and preserving, through laws or other social control mechanisms, the values and the general norms of the system, their consistency, and consequently, ensuring the integration of the social system itself. As with other aspects of the social system, institutions become differentiated and functionally specialized in relation to the particular functional requirements of the subsystems. Therefore, we can distinguish among relational institutions, which define social status and roles, regulatory institutions, which regulate actors' pursuit of their own interests preventing it occurs in a non-functional way for the social system, and, cultural institutions, which are concerned with actors' acceptance of norms and values. Values, norms, collectivity, and roles constitute the structure of the social systems (Williams 1961: 74–76). A *societal community* is a segmented and functionally differentiated system. It becomes aggregated into a complex intertwined set of communities, the latter, in turn, being ruled notwithstanding its internal differentiation, by shared systems of norms and values. The hallmark of a societal community is stable and widespread solidarity; it therefore meets the need for integration of a complex society.

If we distinguish among different action orientations, be they instrumental, expressive or moral, then the term *pattern variable* refers to an action orientation, within social systems or the individual personality, one which constitutes an alternative to another orientation. The overall pattern-variable scheme serves the theoretical purpose of making possible the analysis of the social, the cultural and the personality systems. It also defines a set of dichotomous possibilities, called dilemmas or alternatives, which are inherent to action orientations, and hence, to the relations among social roles. Each alternative corresponds to a particular combination of different and opposed action orientations. Parsons developed what he took to be an exhaustive classification of these:

a. the alternative between affectivity and affective neutrality indicates a dilemma between one's choosing a reward or being subject to discipline;
b. self-orientation or collectivity-orientation corresponds to the alternative between considering one's own interest or that of the collective;

c. the dilemma of universalism vs. particularism is an alternative between one's conforming to norms of general value and forming a *cathectic* attachment orientation towards particular objects (which may also be persons). The actor is therefore not neutral towards them;

d. the choice between achievement and ascription, or quality, shows there is a prevailing consideration of what an actor does or carries out (i.e., his performances), or of some of his peculiar characteristics or stable attributes, such as age, height, social status, and so on;

e. the choice between an actor's specific instrumental or expressive interest, on the one hand, and an interest characterized by a plurality of indistinct orientations, on the other, corresponds to the alternative between specificity and diffusion (Black 1981: 283–286; Johnson 1975: 26–28; Rocher 1974: 36–40).

As Parsons argues, the first three alternatives evidence dilemmas in individual actors' orientations. The fourth and fifth are, by contrast, defined by considering the set of relevant (from the actors' point of view) characteristics of the concerned social objects; these can be other actors with a plurality of orientations of their own. Therefore, reference is no longer made to a single actor, but to the entire set of reciprocal references of all relevant actors. Parsons emphasizes the usefulness of this classification through appropriate examples in studies in which the conceptual apparatus has been, at least partly, applied. The social, cultural, and personality systems can be analyzed from a functional point of view by considering their internal differentiation as well as their requirements for survival and maintaining themselves in a condition of equilibrium, that is to say, for keeping regular relations within the system notwithstanding environmental changes (Williams 1961: 94–95).

If there is a condition of strain which results from defective integration of the system, from a condition in which certain actors cannot work and develop given the constraints imposed upon them by their environment, then there must also be a systemic rebalancing process. The four "features"—or dimensions—of a system are, in a "cybernetic" order (borrowing from Parsons' terminology) from a maximum of energy and a minimum of information to the reverse: adaptation, goal-attainment, integration and concealed pattern maintenance. He considers these features to be *functional imperatives* of every system, that is to say, problems that every system should be able to successfully cope with if it is not to suffer dysfunctional consequences, e.g. internal strains and/or insufficient adaptation to external environments. In Parsons' words, taken together, they form a "four-function paradigm" (Morse 1961: 113–141).

Adaptation means that the social system, and any system in general, conform to requirements imposed by external environments; at the same time, they actively transform them by mobilizing resources for adapting to system requirements. *Goal-attainment* designates the system orientation to specific goals. These can be functional for it alone and so not subordinated to others. They are therefore *ultimate*. *Integration* means that the elements of the social system are reciprocally compatible, and the system is able to maintain internal solidarity and analytically defined boundaries in relation to its external environments. *Latent pattern maintenance*, or *latency*, refers to the problem of preserving, for the social system, actors' motivations, as well as their knowledge, norms and values. All these elements are necessary if it is to sustain itself and undergo integration (Devereux 1961: 56–59; Fox, Lidz, Bershady 2005: 7–9; Johnson 1974: 40–45; Lidz 2000: 403–404; Morse 1961: 113–127).

Parsons considers that the systemic problems of adaptation and goal-attainment are of an instrumental nature. That is, they require the performance of tasks that concern the system as a whole. On the contrary, the problems of integration and latent pattern maintenance require *expressive* system maintenance activities and these, in turn, require the contribution of energies which can resolve strains and reconstruct required abilities (Morse 1961: 114–116). In differentiated systems, systemic integration requires appropriate "generalized symbolic media of interchange" between the systems themselves. With the phrase, "generalized symbolic media of interchange," Parsons actually is referring to instruments of a symbolic nature, such as money or influence, through which the systems that form a general action system are put in mutual relation in keeping with those institutionalized norms which prescribe and regulate its use. An actor's use of one or more media of this kind does not reduce their availability to the other actors. These media are generalized in the sense that interchange between systems can take place in a plurality of pre-established circumstances. In particular, where the social system is concerned, there are specific institutional environments which ensure the development of its integrative and regulatory functions (Prandini 1998: 61–62).

Insufficient systemic integration leads to strains and causes social change. Social change takes on an "evolutionary" character in differentiated societies. Those which consist of subsystems and are distinguished from one another by their unique characteristics and functional importance are characterized in this way. A process of social change is *evolutionary* when the elements of the social and cultural systems are separated from one another. They can therefore be studied as independent units. *Evolutionary universals* are the evolutionary processes that can be found in several systems which operate under different conditions. They therefore have the potential to be of the greatest relevance in the process of building systems—social systems, in particular. The latter are capable of conforming, over the long run, to the functional needs of their environments through processes of adaptive upgrading.

Adaptation to external environments and subsystem integration assume the use of generalized interchange media. It is through these media that *cybernetic mechanisms* automatically adapt to external environments and thereby allow for the continuous flow of communication and reciprocal equilibrium between, on the one hand, those systems which provide meanings and information (e.g. the cultural system), and, on the other hand, those which provide them with energy. Non-social systems, such as living organisms, are a case in point. In a cybernetic control hierarchy (i.e. one characterized by automatic reciprocal adaptation), the systems that provide meanings and information control those which provide energy, but they are conditioned by them as far as their ability to adapt to their environments. The *human condition*, conceived as a system, has a structure which contains four interconnected elements.

In the first place, there is the natural environment, which provides lifeless resources. In the second place, there is the human organic system, which makes possible a particular capacity to adapt to the environment. In the third place, there is the general action system; it is provided with peculiar cognitive and symbolic abilities and develops knowledge of the environment and makes normative evaluations. The general system of action comprises four systems placed at a lower analytic level: the cultural system, the social system, the personality system, and the organism. Finally, Parsons analytically identifies the *telic system*. Through this, the social system and the human beings that make it up and engage in their various interactions, are assigned fundamental meanings and value orientations (among Parsons' interpreters on this point are Hamilton 1989: 159–168; Johnson 1975: 40–45; Rocher 1974: 50–51, 70–73).

CONCLUDING REMARKS

In this introduction, we have presented a part of the complex conceptual apparatus used by Parsons. The definitions given have been drawn from his works and refer to the following concepts: theory, action, social action, action scheme or system, reference frame, theory of action, paradigms, social, cultural and personality system, functions, role, process, social structure, collectivity, values, institutions, pattern variables, functional imperatives, four-feature paradigm, adaptation, goal attainment, integration, latency, generalized symbolic media of interchange, evolutionary universals, adaptive upgrading, cybernetic mechanisms, the human condition, general action systems, telic system.

Chapter Two

The First Period (1928–1937)

Parsons' first period is characterized by his focus on themes of economic sociology such as the German debate on the definition, origin and the development of capitalism. Themes related to social science theory and epistemology, with particular reference to the concepts of the ideal type, social action and institution, also appear in this period. They had previously been dealt with by several representatives of the contemporary European social sciences, and Parsons committed to studying their works in depth during his extended stays in England and Germany. These studies laid the theoretical foundations for his entire production of that period, starting from his first essay (late 1920s), *Capitalism in Recent German Literature*, which dates back to the late 1920s (Parsons 1928; 1929).

This essay, published by a journal on political economy as evidence of the author's economic education, intended to present the thought of Sombart and Weber in condensed form. It consists of two parts. In the first, which centers on Sombart's production, in particular, on his most famous work, *Modern Capitalism*, Parsons outlines its main purpose. He introduces and defines this theoretical subject from both a conceptual and a sociological and historical point of view and also gives his evaluation of it. In this connection, he remarks that Sombart's unit of analysis, namely capitalism, is arbitrarily formulated without regard for the historical changes it has undergone, and that the scientific quality of Sombart's production is affected by his determinist metaphysical assumption that capitalism is the result of the action of a Spirit whose evolution would follow a law of its own.

By contrast to this, the second part of this work focuses on Weber. It considers both his epistemological and historical-sociological works, especially those which concern modern capitalism and the rationality that defines it. Parsons argues that the Weberian ideal type includes two different concepts,

9

a general one in which the concept of capitalism can be used as a widely applicable instrument for selecting and analyzing certain specific historical events, and another that instead can be applied only to some particular historical objects such a modern capitalism. Calling both concepts "ideal types" can give rise to confusion, according to Parsons, because it is not always clear whether Weber intends to refer to capitalism in general, or to modern capitalism in particular.

In subsequent years, Parsons ceased to focus exclusively on the theme of capitalism, but instead turned his attention to the theory and epistemology of the social sciences. A first result of this was an essay entitled *Prolegomena to a Theory of Social Institutions*. As the title indicates, it included introductory remarks on a theory of institutions. Although this essay dates back to 1934, it remained unpublished for a long time (Parsons 1990). Parsons there identifies two different ways to study an institution, one subjective and the other objective, these being defined from either the point of view of the individual who relates to the institutions, or from a sociologist's point of view. In the first case, the subject pursues his aims while taking the available media into account, but his actions are restrained by the technological, economic and political context in which he operates. Actions occur within a system of norms and values. As a consequence, the subjective way in which an institution is studied primarily focuses on the relation between an individual, on the one hand, and the social institutions and the leading norms and values of his or her society, on the other. The latter forms, a moral community that binds the individual at the same time as it remains external to him or her.

In the second case, a sociologist's point of view is adopted. Accordingly, Parsons takes into account the fact that individuals do not act separately but, rather, in relation to one another, and are bound by common norms in the form of laws and customs. Institutions are then a system of interdependent regulatory norms. The level of integration of an institution depends on the degree to which single institutions harmoniously relate to one another. Determining this is an empirical problem.

Parsons' first work, *The Structure of Social Action*, dates back to 1937. It required lengthy preparation. In the course of its development, his thinking matured thanks to his stays in England and Germany. It deepened still further during the first years in which he taught at Harvard (Camic 1991). There he once again took up his interest in Weber and in the themes of capitalism and the social institutions. Moreover, for the first time, he tried to reconstruct some fundamental theses concerning social action on the basis of on certain classical authors such as Marshall, Pareto, Durkheim and Weber himself. Parsons' preliminary remarks indicate that his work is intended to be empirical as it makes constant reference to the works of these four authors. His analysis starts from the concept of *action rationality*: any action in which the means used by the actor conform to the pursued ends with an empirically assessable probability is rational. This assumes that certain conditions are external to the actor, and so not within his control. These conditions are relevant not only to the actor, but also to others. In fact, the actor has to take them into account in order to pursue his ends and others must do so in order to understand its course.

External conditions can exert a merely random influence over action because they result from factors such as genetic heritage or environment which cannot be controlled by the actor. In contrast to this, the influence of norms on action is not random, and therefore represents a source of order for the actor. External conditions and normative order jointly form the initial condition in which an action is carried out. The situation differs in some aspects which the actor considers important, from a future state of the things which he anticipates and judges desirable, and toward which he orients his action. The positivist theory of action gives importance to external conditions, that is to say, to the objective elements the actor considers random and uncontrollable. This also applies to the utilitarian theory, which takes in to account only the relation which exists between media and ends, and does not ask about these ends. Therefore, according to this theory, the actor is motivated by what he or she takes to be his contingent interest. According to utilitarians and positivists ends are random. By contrast to this, an idealist theory assigns importance to normative factors which have a symbolic yet subjective meaning for the actor.

Parsons' *voluntaristic* theory of action is distinguished from the aforementioned theories by the fact that it assumes the existence of an independent actor who: 1) acts in the absence of determining, external factors, such as genetic heritage or environment 2) nonetheless takes them into account in pursuing his ends, and who 3) though motivated by norms, he does not limit himself to expressing them through his action because he interprets them from his own point of view. His action, considered in its basic elements (actor, media, ends, external conditions, normative orientation), constitutes the unit act. The actor can combine different actions and so create complex action systems which have separate or "emerging properties"—and this in contrast to elementary actions. The actors, the action they carry out, and the media which they use do not, however, concretely exist. Rather, they are abstract concepts formulated for analytical purposes.

In their pursuit of ends, the actors (defined in abstracto) make use of the various means which they control in the most effective way possible based on their knowledge and beliefs. Still, these may not coincide with objectively valid beliefs. The means which he or she chooses do, however, conform to the existing normative order as it is viewed from his or her point of view. Action is restrained by objective external factors as they appear to the actor; it is also guided by the normative order where the choice of the ends is concerned, the latter being subjective. Since ends are chosen willingly, hence Parsons' term "voluntaristic." He aims at showing how Marshall, Pareto, Durkheim and Weber have contributed, though perhaps not deliberately, to the development of such a voluntaristic theory of action. To evidence the theoretical convergence among these authors, he makes use of a conceptual pattern which conforms to the principle of "analytical realism." In keeping with this principle, he uses concepts in this theoretical study for the purpose of formulating a theory of action.

Therefore, they do not correspond to real phenomena, i.e., do not literally and directly represent reality, but are instead formulated for the purpose of defining certain elements of the system of thought that are to be analytically distinguished from the others. They aim to produce a generally applicable theoretical pattern a *generalized system of action*, to be used to understand any really existing phenomenon. This theoretical pattern includes several distinct elements. First there are external conditions (heritage and environment). These are intended by the subject to be the means and pre-established conditions of action, and also a potential source of ignorance and error. Secondly, there is a set of interconnected means and ends. Thirdly, there is a consistent set of ultimate values. Finally, there is a factor, which relates the conditional and normative elements of action. This consists of the effort through which norms are turned into practices, external conditioning factors notwithstanding.

Parsons acknowledges the presence of these conceptual and theoretical elements, or at least of some of them, in the works of Marshall, Pareto, Durkheim and Weber, regardless of terminological and theoretical differences. For him, such differences are of minor importance compared to the points they have in common. As a matter of fact, none of these authors is committed to the positivist theory of action, nor to the idealist theory. On the contrary, they contribute, each in his or her own way, to the development of an analytical and theoretical pattern, which goes beyond this distinction, selects significant elements from reality. It can also be used to observe and describe facts that are relevant to empirical research, which, in turn, leads to an integrated and consistent body of knowledge. Parsons dwells at length on Durkheim and Weber. In his view, the convergence of their thought on main theoretical points is greater than that of the other two authors; for they both seem to pay greater attention to the way in which norms provide an orientation to action. Both Durkheim and Weber seem to focus to a greater extent on the relevance of norms when assessing the mutual relation between norms and value attitudes, on the one hand, and between religious ideas and rituals, on the other.

The properties emerging from such action systems are to be found at three different levels of abstraction. These are the object of the disciplines of economics, politics and sociology. Sociology, in particular, now has an analytical and theoretical pattern at its disposal, through which it is possible to make progress in this field. Weber's contribution to this derives first and foremost from the fact that he formulated the analytical elements of the voluntaristic theory of action. These elements can be either directly or indirectly inferred from the ideal-type conceptual pattern. He would, however, not have been able to distinguish (in a way that was desirable to Parsons) between two different types of motivation, the first being that of actors who act in the real world, the second that of abstract actors, whose action can be understood as a set of situated meanings not defined in space-time. This second kind of motivation is particularly relevant to an analysis of social action.

CONCLUDING REMARKS

In this period (1928–1937), Parsons devoted himself to in-depth studies of certain classical authors in the field of sociology, e.g. Pareto, Durkheim and Weber, and also to the study of the works of economists like Marshall. His purpose was to formulate a conceptual pattern through which social action could be described and explained. That he was interested in the work of these authors is clear from some early essays in which he introduced and commented on Sombart's and Weber's works on the origins of modern capitalism; it is also evidenced in his subsequent theoretical research, where he distinguishes two different methods (subjective and objective) for studying institutions. In his first book, *The Structure of Social Action*, Parsons points to a convergence between the texts of these authors where the formulation of an implicit theory of action is concerned, that is, a theory in which the constitutive elements of action (actor, means, ends, external conditions, and normative orientation) are analytically defined. Action itself, which forms the unit of analysis, or *unit act,* is voluntaristic. It is not determined by external factors such as heritage and environment, but rather carried out by actors who are guided by norms and in keeping with their own interpretation of them.

Chapter Three

The Second Period (1938–1963)

Parsons' "empirical" production of this period, which focuses on democracy and related problems in Germany during the years of the Weimar Republic (1920s and early 1930s), and also those of the United States during the early 1950s, is quite interesting. However, we prefer to overlook it for the time being and concentrate instead on his theoretical production. Proceeding to formulate a unitary theory of social action, i.e. one that does not conceive of action merely as an effect of heritage and environment, he attempts to systematically explore the theoretical implications of the concepts of action and social norm. One consequence of this is an enrichment of his conceptual apparatus. It is achieved through a revision of the concepts of norm and institution, and through the formulation of new ones: function, personality, internalization, and social system. These are still further developed in his subsequent works. This period is also characterized by the study of the social structure and the social system, an area which had previously been neglected. (Hamilton 1989: 110).

A TRANSITIONAL WORK

The transition between these two periods is marked by a work entitled *Actor, Situation and Normative Pattern*. In this study, which dates back to 1939 but was not published until the 1980s, Parsons continued to focus on the concepts of actor, situation and cultural model. At this point, however, he began to attempt to fulfill a purpose he had never previously pursued, namely, the formulation of a structural-functional theory of the social system (Parsons 1986; see also Wenzel 1986). This essay deals first with some of the themes he had already tackled in *The Structure of Social Action*. These include: a distinction

14

between the conceptual apparatuses of biology and theory of action; a theoretical framework in which actor and situation are placed in mutual relation; and a typology of the actor's modes of orientation. These are, in turn, distinguished into cognitive, teleological (that is to say, purposive) and affective orientations. The cognitive and the teleological modes of orientation refer to objects such as notions, purposes, norms, and are external to the actor; by contrast to this, the affective orientation is specifically subjective, and has two components. On the one hand, it is marked by positive and negative stimuli, on the other, it entails a moral evaluation. A situation resulting from interactive processes among the actors forms the object of their orientations. These orientations may be of a cognitive, teleological, affective (i.e., *cathectic*) nature, the latter term being used here for the first time by Parsons. If cathectic, they may also be of a social nature, as when several actors participate in a situation.

In the case of the latter, the actor's action can be either a condition, a medium, or an instrument of exchange, coercion or influence for other actors, or vice versa. A merely instrumental orientation toward others is countered by moral considerations. They make reference to abstract normative patterns, even though moral judgments are usually related to actions and qualities of real persons. These normative models meet the integration requirements of the social system, which cannot tolerate an uncontrolled manifestation of individual interests, affections and impulses. Social integration involves an actor knowing clearly and precisely which of the existing criteria are normative, and taking them into account in his or her actions. The stability of the social system depends on the integration of individual personalities, amongst other factors. This, in turn, involves a sufficient degree of coordination among actors' different modes of orientation, as well as among the different resulting action trends. A common normative pattern can meet these requirements as they are expressed by the social system.

The integration of individuals into the social system takes place either through the order created by social stratification, or through an authority that legitimizes positions within the social system, or through the definition of social roles that are capable of stabilizing individual actions. The personality system is divided into action subsystems. These have to functionally conform to the specific context of individual acts, and consequently to the actor's situation, to the goals he or she sets, to the normative and expressive standards guiding his behavior, and to the action system as a whole. The social system is functionally differentiated into roles, though only some of them are necessary to its continuity (system differentiation into roles connected to the actors' age would, for example, be excluded). For social actors, role performance involves a division of work, to which there corresponds functional differentiation and specialization within the social system.

The differentiation of the social system is distinguished from the functional differentiation of individual activities and roles. To provide a functionally appropriate solution to the problem of order and integration, the social system must divide itself up into various institutions, formal organizations and systems of juridical norms. Institutions stabilize and sanction expectations based on norms. Formal organizations place actors in relation to the groups with which they interact; they cause them to depend on an authority and to act in accord with normative patterns. Juridical norms form a systematic body of laws that constrain the action of groups. This conceptual pattern can be used to provide an explanation of, and a systematic reflection on, actual empirical problems.

THE SOCIAL SYSTEM AND
TOWARD A GENERAL THEORY OF ACTION

These two important works, both of which were published in 1951, will be jointly considered here. The latter develops some themes dealt with by the former, such as action categories, system, role, personality, value orientations, institution, but does not introduce any new themes. In these works, Parsons sets some theoretical objectives for himself. First, he aims to develop a conceptual pattern in an effort to identify and describe the constitutive elements of the social system. The latter is intended as a set of actions which are organized through roles and carried out by a plurality of individuals. Roles are interdependent. They maintain their continuous reciprocal orientation, and consequently, their internal pattern. This pattern is put into a changeable relation with the environment, because the environment itself is changeable. His second objective is to analyze the mechanisms that provide the social actors with the motivations for acting according to the social roles and the norms that govern their behaviors. Finally, these works aim to study processes of change which are internal to the social system. Parsons dwells at length on the first two objectives, whereas the theme of change itself is dealt with in the final chapters of these works.

The social system strictly relates to the cultural system (i.e. an organized system of norms, values and symbols). There is indeed a dominant system of values which allows for the integration of single individuals into the social system, even if this system is subject to modification as a result of the need for compromise which is imposed on individuals by contingent situations. Hence, the integration of individuals into the social system and their internalization of the dominant system of values are never lacking (the social system would otherwise not exist), yet they are always imperfect. Furthermore, the social system is strictly related to the personality system (i.e. an organized system of need dispositions), since there is a correspondence (albeit also imperfect) between the categories of the social system, (e.g. age, gender or ethnic group), and the ways in which the actor classifies him or herself.

The social system distinguishes itself from the cultural and the personality systems by the fact that it is made up of roles which are performed by individuals or communities concerned with this task. Roles are institutionalized in part. This means that those who act in the system form a collectivity, have internalized common values, and are subject to obligations and prohibitions. To perform any social role, actors must be in possession of *facilities*, be they of a material or symbolic nature. These can be granted to them either through a decision made by an authority, or through institutionalized rules, or through a competitive process. Furthermore, roles can provide a solution to problems concerning an actor's interaction with others, and they differ depending on the kind of interaction involved. Problems may be instrumental, expressive or integrative. Actors impose their particular orientation on the system. This orientation can be either cognitive (as when the aspects of a situation that are significant for the actor are defined), or *cathectic* (as when they concern the relevance an actor attributes to those objects to which he or she addresses himself or herself) or *evaluative* (as when an actor selects the aspects he or she considers relevant).

The actors orient themselves towards a future situation which they symbolically anticipate. They may wish to control the situation by acting instrumentally toward some end, or by meeting a need disposition or conforming to a normative orientation. This orientation is put at his disposal by the cultural system. The motivation to act results from the personality system and relates to the normative and the social systems via specific mechanisms. An action system is perfectly integrated if the systems that constitute it, namely, the social, the cultural and the personality systems, create an orderly set of interdependent parts, and if this set of parts remains distinct from its environment. The equilibrium that comes to characterize such an action system can be either static or dynamic.

The constitutive elements of the social system, understood as a network of interactive relations, are: the social act, the types of status held and the roles performed within the social act, and the actor himself; the latter is a social reference unit for status and roles. Each social system should meet some functional prerequisites, or "imperatives," in order to persist as an orderly set of elements, irrespective of either system stability or change. These prerequisites include biological imperatives (the fulfillment of which allows for the maintenance and continuation of individual life), psychological-social imperatives (the conditions through which it is possible to achieve a minimum of personality stability), and systemic prerequisites (the conditions through which a sufficient number of actors are properly motivated to participate in the social system and refrain from socially destructive deviant behaviors). The order of a system, and so also its stability, depend on the degree to which actors' motivations are consistent with (or "integrated" into) the prevailing normative standards and the value orientations.

Shared norms and values provide the prerequisite for this integration, based on which a group of actors becomes integrated, i.e., forms a collectivity. Norms and values orient the actors within the institutions they establish by shaping roles and related behavioral expectations. Actors orient themselves to the objects that belong to a social system, and in particular, to other actors, in a cognitive, *cathectic* or evaluative way, and also attach to an instrumental or expressive orientation to their actions. One or another of these modes of orientation is chosen according to priorities established by the cultural system. If the actors act within the institutions they create, they must internalize their value orientation. Socially acquired needs which have become actors' need dispositions can be thus determined in a social system. This system, in turn, establishes the values and defines the norms that constitute a particular institution. Cultural institutions, therefore, are always part of a social system, along with other institutions which define actors' reciprocal role expectations and set the limits within which pursuing private interests is deemed legitimate.

Parsons maintains that for each level of generalization there is contained within the instrumental, expressive or moral orientation of each actor to social roles a limited and fixed number of institutionally established alternatives. The social structure changes depending on the alternatives, (i.e. *pattern variables*) for which the actors demonstrate a preference in their orientations to roles performed within a social system. This preference results from customary choices, and such choices express culture as the actors have internalized it. It also conforms to the definitions and prescriptions of the social roles and to the value standards. First of all, there are two sets of alternatives for expressive and moral orientations. Actors may either want to obtain satisfaction or some type of reward straightaway, or they may renounce them in favor of instrumental interests or moral concerns (affectivity or affective neutrality). Moreover, the actors can pursue their own private interests, or those which they shares with the other members of their collectivity. The choice of one option or another is particularly important for analyzing how much space is left to individuals for pursuing their own private interests, and, also, for understanding the extent of their obligations to the collectivity. The alternative of universalism vs. particularism requires a choice between the types of values that are enforced in role expectations. In contrast to a particularist orientation, a universalistic orientation leads the actors to disregard their relation with particular actors or other social subjects, to discriminate neither in their favor nor to their detriment, but to always maintain the same sort of orientation toward them.

More specifically, the dilemmas of affectivity vs. affective neutrality, orientation to oneself vs. orientation to the collectivity, and universalism vs. particularism, imply that actors have to make choices, and, consequently, that are cognizant of their value orientations. Achievement vs. ascription (or quality) and specificity vs. diffuseness disregard the point of view of the particular actor and instead assume that there are objectively existing alternatives in the social system to which the actor relates. In the case of set of concepts achievement vs. ascription, what is at issue is the particular qualities or attributes of the object to which the actors orients themselves also, these can be permanently attributed to that social object (ascription or quality). Examples are social status, age and degree of kinship. This can also concern performances to be attributed to others with whom the actor has established a relation based on reciprocity of roles. If so, then all that the actor has done becomes relevant to the situation, be it in the area of achievement or performance. With the other pair of concepts, specificity vs. diffuseness, the alternative is between a specific interest of an instrumental or expressive nature (for example, in a professional relation), or a general one the latter not being clearly defined by obligations governing precise social roles. Affective or erotic relations, in which performance reciprocity is not, and cannot be calculated, are a case in point.

Pattern-variables can systematically relate to one another if they are considered within the more general context of the theory of action. In so far as he concentrates first on instrumental orientation, the actor relates to others in a different way, i.e., in a way which depends on the roles he or she performs from time to time. If the action orientation is expressive, then the actors must turn to others, be they individuals or collectivities. On the right occasions, the actors must show an appropriate attachment to them and be receptive towards them, and finally, must correspond to their attitudes in a manner appropriate to the terms of the relation. An expressive orientation may not match an instrumental or moral one; similarly, these may not match each other. Furthermore, a combination of heterogeneous orientations may lead to instability. It is however possible to provide some examples of a classification of different kinds of fusion or separation in the elements of the instrumental and expressive orientation. For example, the fusion of several specific expressive orientation interests can lead to an intense attachment to a particular social object (e.g., a beloved person), and consequently, to the pure role type of romantic love; or, it can lead to an abstract cultural object, such as universal love in a religious sense. Specific performances of an instrumental nature are instead separated both from expressive orientation, and also from the other elements of instrumental orientation.

Actors' motivations and the cultural elements that define them, such as norms and values, cause social relations to be arranged according to roles. An actor orients himself to a social object, particularly in relation to another actor, either because the social object belongs to a class of objects considered significant (i.e. in the case of a classification standard), or because it is significant in itself for the actor (i.e., in the case of a relational standard). The alternative between achievement and ascription is relevant for classifying actors among the various types of status and roles that form the social system, and to differentiate them within their environment. Systemic solidarity is shown by the actors' common value orientation, and consequently by the prevalence of one of their orientations to the collectivity, assuming that system solidarity itself is considered a value. The predominant orientations in a collectivity (universalism vs. particularism, achievement vs. ascription, and so on) combine to provide the social system with certain points of reference. Pattern-variables are therefore used to analyze the structural elements of the social system.

In particular, the dilemmas of affectivity vs. affective neutrality, and specificity vs. diffuseness are relevant where an orientation to action in the personality system is concerned. By contrast to this, the dilemmas of universalism vs. particularism, and ascription vs. achievement, are relevant as regards the predominant value orientation in the cultural system. Finally, the dilemma of orientation to oneself vs. orientation to the collectivity is internal to the social system in the sense that it can be useful to its integration. These five dilemmas, jointly considered, have the value orientation of the social system as an object. Their analytical distinction can be also used to classify kinds of social structures. In fact, actually existing social structures are the result of combining value orientations with the other elements of the social system.

The social system differentiates itself both in terms of roles and in terms of distribution of status and roles in a given social structure. Each social system is provided with mechanisms for distributing among the actors all that they need to achieve their purposes, even though the actors have a fixed number of opportunities due to the limitations on their resources. The presence of material and symbolic rewards can promote relations based on loyalty between one actor and others when these rewards are institutionalized. Where norms are enforced by a legitimate authority, institutionalization limits the pursuit of private interests, and consequently, the orientation to oneself; at the same time, it promotes the orientation to interests or purposes that concern the collectivity. Institutions are a source of structural differentiation within the social system. Through classification of the existing institutions it is possible to connect the various parts of the social system and comparatively analyze different social structures.

It is possible to formulate a general pattern of classification which includes only some clusterings of those pattern variables which are empirically verifiable. Parsons discusses four kinds of clustering at some length: kinship systems, stratification structures, power systems, and institutionalized religion. Societies must meet functional requirements, hence the restricted number of empirically existing social structures. These requirements are, on the one hand, the conditions that ensure stability and duration to a social system ("universal imperatives"). On the other hand, there are also compatibility imperatives which limit the simultaneous presence of different structural elements in the same society. These elements, an example of which is provided by kinship systems and occupational role systems, result from stable patterns of action orientation and the situation to which actors become oriented.

In addition to social structure, other structures contribute to the institutionalization of the prevailing pattern of values in a society. Inscriptive standards are relevant because they allow for the organization of kinship units into wider structures, such as communities, ethnic groups and social classes. Achievement standards are relevant when an actor's universalistic orientation to the collectivity becomes established. And, even though the variable of "orientation to oneself or to the collectivity "is important for social integration (which occurs only when the second alternative prevails), others become relevant because they designate particular kinds of social structure. The modern social structure that is termed "industrial" (the only one compatible with capitalistic development) is marked by universalistic (rather than particularistic), specific (rather than widespread), affective (rather than neutral) orientations, and it is achievement-oriented (rather than ascription-oriented) in its assignment of roles. For each of these aspects, this kind of structure is different than others. A case in point would be the Chinese imperial bureaucratic social structure of the Mandarin age.

Once complementary role expectations have been established, they can be maintained without any particular effort unless two tendencies become realized: in the first place, an actor may not correctly or sufficiently learn the contents of role behaviors, or may not be motivated to put them into effect. This is an indication that his socialization process has not been effective. Secondly, an actor may depart from norms and thereby produce problems, or even activate learning and social control mechanisms. The latter keep the system balanced and their defective functioning can generate tensions in the social and the personality systems. However, the process of internalizing social norms does not only work through rewards and punishments. Also relevant are the interaction with the socialization agent, its imitation, the identification with it, and consequently, the internalization of its values.

It is through socialization that we become oriented toward values. This value orientation contributes to the formation of the basic structure of the personality. To a great extent, it is also a function of the fundamental structure of roles and the prevailing system of values. The structure and the functioning process of personality and of the social system cannot be identical given the differences which exist among individuals, the varying outcomes of the secularization process, and the existence of alternative ways of performing social roles. A deviant orientation is revealed by an actor's motivations. It results from his socially acquired need dispositions, and causes him or her to infringe one or more normative patterns and thus disturb the equilibrium of society's interactive processes. Some compromises are however possible and even quite probable, such as cases in which a subject has ambivalent reactions toward the ruling systems of norms and values. Deviant tendencies are not, in and of themselves, problematic, but are to be understood in relation to particular, mutually complementary role expectations, and to situations the actor can encounter.

The kind of deviance that most endangers the social system relates to persons whose relations are incompatible with the systemic and impersonal values of efficiency and performance. Strains result when individuals have difficulty conforming to normative expectations or correctly interpreting them. Strains also flow from the fact that institutions have difficulties in sanctioning infringements, and exerting effective social control in situations of uncertainty. A conflict of roles generates inner conflicts and these are exacerbated where institutional roles become a point of contention. The social marginalization of vagrants, or the status of the sick person are, respectively, deviant and non-deviant individual solutions to such tensions. By contrast to this, the development of criminal gangs is a collective, deviant solution to a socially induced condition of strain. The search for scapegoats (which reveals itself particularly in anti-Semitism) diverges from the previous form of deviance by the fact that some actors seek to legitimate their aggressive actions. This attempted claim to legitimacy then comes to be accepted by the collectivity to which they belong. The genesis and the consequences of deviance can be therefore studied using the already known conceptual apparatus which is employed in the analysis of social systems. Processes of social control are put into effect in order to prevent and counter deviant tendencies and the conditions that produce them in individuals and collectivities, so also to put an end to structural strains and rebalance interactive processes.

In summary, we can state that:

a. The functional problems of conformity and deviance are inherent in the social systems, given the aforementioned characteristics of the cultural systems.
b. Deviance and social control processes begin with the first socialization process and continue throughout the life of the subject.
c. Any inconsistency between the structure of individual need dispositions and the role system gives rise to systemic strains, and these promote a tendency to deviance.
d. This tendency is strengthened by the existing gaps in the social control system, but it is countered by some individual psychological mechanisms.
e. When tendencies to deviance resulting from the social structure are not controlled by social control mechanisms, they become one of the major causes of social change.

Bearing in mind that culture provides the criteria for action orientation, the interdependence between the cultural system and the social system can be studied considering the action systems (and consequently, the cognitive, *cathectic* and evaluative action orientation) in their relation to the systems of ideas (beliefs, expressive symbols and value orientations). In addition to value orientations, the systems of shared beliefs, such as scientific knowledge, ideologies and religious ideas, are elements of the cultural system. Religious ideas, which are of a non-empirical nature, serve an additional social function, namely, to answer existential questions. When empirical beliefs are institutionalized, they can be distinguished into either pure or applied scientific knowledge and ideologies. Scientific knowledge is characterized by its strong universalistic orientation. Finally, ideologies' claim to truth (a claim which the social sciences can question) and provide values with a generalized cognitive legitimacy. The latter may be completely or partly deviant; similarly for the patterns of orientation towards them.

Non-empirical beliefs, religious beliefs in particular, become part of the empirical world to the extent that a system of beliefs is institutionalized. There are therefore strains and contradictions within this system, and it is marked by unstable equilibrium. This has consequences for the social system: in fact, actors receive knowledge, rewards, values and orientations to action from the system of beliefs. Expressive interests take part in the cultural system because they discover in it their symbolic manifestation. This occurs through meanings that are an object of reward, *cathexis* (attachment) and normative evaluation for the actors. The meanings of symbolic acts, whatever their content may be, are communicated during interactive processes and therefore become sources of orientation for the actors. Relevant alternatives for the transmission of meanings consist in affectivity vs. neutral affectivity, and specificity vs. diffuseness. Institutionalization and the consequent creation of social roles stabilize the symbolic system and the cultural system in general, thereby making possible the transmission of organized meanings.

The symbolic element is implicit in social actors' orientations to physical and cultural objects as this occurs in keeping with standards of affectivity and specificity (where actors' specific interests are separate from their relational context), standards of affectivity and diffuseness (where actors' interests merge into an abstract cultural object, such as love for the human kind), standards of affective neutrality and specificity (an example of which is solidarity, which includes an expectation of an expressive orientation distinct from a given context and one that has become institutionalized), standards of affective neutrality and diffuseness (when diffuseness prevails, expressive interests merge and are subordinated to non-specific instrumental considerations. Examples include relations in which the desire for approval and esteem is important). Modern medical practice provides a picture of the types of relations which can develop among the elements of the social system. Illness is, in fact, a condition of trouble, partly biologically and partly socially defined, for the normally functioning individual; it is therefore also a condition of trouble for the social system. The doctor's role is institutionalized. It requires a great deal of technical competence and implies that the professional has strong control over his or her own (and others') anxieties concerning death. As the professional codes of conduct emphasize, this is oriented toward the patients' collectivity and is marked by personal disinterestedness, affective neutrality, universalism and specificity as regards the relation with patients themselves.

There is also a set of institutionalized expectations for patients. Patients are exempted from usual responsibilities, depending of the nature and the seriousness of their illness. Their condition does not depend on their will, and they are therefore not responsible for it. Still, it is a source of strain on them and their family. The patients are obligated to try to recover their health and to find a technically competent help for this purpose. Their role is oriented to the doctors' collectivity in the sense that they are obliged to cooperate with the doctors for the joint purpose of regaining their health. Institutionalizing expectations for the roles of both doctors and patients has several purposes. It makes the doctors' performance of their role more effective, but also more acceptable for the patients and their families, and it helps the family to successfully face the psychological strains produced by the condition of illness.

To summarize, two theoretical problems have been dealt with in our discussion of *The Social System* so far. First, there was the development of a conceptual pattern aimed at identifying and describing the major elements that constitute the social system. This was done by delineating their interrelations. Secondly, there was the analysis of motivational processes which originate in the personalities of the individual actors and in the contingent situations in which they act, but can impact upon the social system in a number of ways. The theme of social change is dealt with in the last part of *The Social System* and in *Toward a General Theory of Action*. Parsons thus maintains his focus on the concept of system. His discussion of it in these works presumes his earlier development of it. The processes of change either within the system, or to the system itself, are relevant here. The social system consists of interactive and reciprocally-oriented processes. Its equilibrium can only be maintained if the actors have acquired, through the socialization process, the necessary orientations for perfuming their roles, and if social control mechanisms have been activated to offset motivations for deviant behaviors. Thus Parsons' theory of systems aims to analyze the conditions under which a system either changes or maintains its stability. Orientation to values and their acquisition through the socialization process allow for formulation of the mechanisms by which change is produced. Parsons' position on this changed in subsequent years, because he did not here formulate a theory of action which could explain social change.

The presence of strains on the social system, as these result from the actors' imperfect integration of need dispositions in the cultural system, implies a process of rebalancing not only for the actors, but also for the social system itself. Indeed, actors must internalize and express new value patterns, and the system must provide mechanisms capable of contending with the strains which they cause. As concerns the social system, change has its origins in the cultural system, more precisely, it is caused by changes occurring in the subsystems of beliefs, expressive symbols and values. In the final part of his work, Parsons recalls that he has availed himself of the concept of system as a principle for organizing and guiding his research. The theoretical treatment of this theme required him to focus on institutionalization of cultural patterns, particularly those which are the foundation for value orientation, and also on the internalized processes through which the actors acquire motivations to perform the roles that make up the social system. Parsons emphasizes that the theory of action includes theories of personality, culture, the social system and the relations among these systems. Sociological theory distinguishes itself from economic theory, from social psychology and from the other social sciences because it takes into account a variety of organizational levels for rational action, and also because its theoretical-conceptual apparatus is sufficiently specific.

OTHER THEORETICAL WORKS
DEVELOPED DURING THIS PERIOD

In this second period, after 1951 (the publication year of *The Social System* and *Toward a General Theory of Action*), Parsons wrote additional theoretical works. Some have general theoretical content, e.g., *Working Papers in the Theory of Action* (co-authored with Bales and Shils) and *An Outline of the Social System*. Others, e.g, *The Marshall Lectures* and *Economy and Society*, deal with themes from economic sociology from a theoretical point of view. In all of these works, Parsons introduced some elements which were novel in comparison to those contained in the earlier titles. He formulated a conceptual pattern, the so-called "AGIL scheme," and introduced the category of generalized media of interchange. Though the pattern-variable frame was not abandoned at this point, (see Parsons 1953: 66–67; Parsons, Bales, Shils 1953: 179–190), Parsons judged it appropriate to focus upon the "AGIL scheme." The connection between the pattern-variable frame and the "AGIL scheme" is mentioned in a contribution (published in 1960, but reprinted some years later) (Parsons 1969a). It was written by Parsons in response to Robert Dubin's objection that the two conceptual patterns differed in content (Dubin 1960).

As Parsons argues in this work, both schemes can be used to classify action elements and so have the same theoretical aim. However, the pattern-variable frame is considered insufficient because it limits itself to defining an action system. It only analyzes how the actor orients himself in relation to a situation, and how the objects he considers significant (where they are characterized by specificity, affectivity, universalism, etc.) present themselves. The combination of these objects defines the way in which the actor acts. The pattern-variables frame cannot classify actors and objects into kinds. In fact, it does not place both the actor and the relevant objects in a stable system of institutionalized norms, where these norms are characterized by a set of rules and procedures that can be analytically identified and, taken together, form the environment of the action system.

The four functional subsystems indicated by the acronym AGIL, which form the system of institutionalized norms, can instead provide this classification of actors and relevant objects. In so far as it is implemented, it can also point to systemic conditions of internal stability and identify the ways in which the system relates to the environment. Each element of the alternatives mentioned in the pattern-variable frame (e.g. specificity vs. diffuseness) is included in a single subsystem. This explains how the pattern-variable frame is analytically included in the AGIL pattern. It also makes it clear that the presence and combinations of these variables in the AGIL system is not random at all, but incorporates the normative order of the system. This order presumes that the system can conform to the external environment formed by organisms, personalities and cultural systems, and so interact with it. Since the time it was introduced into his work the AGIL scheme continued to be a core issue for the Parsons. The concepts of personality and social system were further developed in order to illustrate their theoretical potentials. He also pointed out some general conditions which ensure the equilibrium of the social system. Finally, Parsons also wrote some essays through which he intended to develop a theoretical basis for economic sociology within the general context of a theory of the social system.

Among these essays, the most famous is the monograph *Economy and Society*, co-authored with Neil J. Smelser (Parsons, Smelser 1957). We shall first mention the general theoretical works of the second period (those published after 1951). We shall then focus on *Economy and Society*, along with some other works also dealing with economic sociology. The continuity of all these together with others from the same period, in particular *The Social System*, is both thematic and theoretical. The theories of action, the personality, the cultural and the social systems, the conceptual relations among these systems, and that of equilibrium and change to the social system, continue to be the main object of Parsons' interest. This continuity is also partly conceptual. In fact, the themes he addresses and the constitutive elements of the social structure (roles, collectivity, values, norms) are outlined and defined in a similar way. The constitutive elements of personality (Parsons retains the well-known classification made by Freud (Ego, Superego, Id)), are, however, examined in greater depth.

Due to their importance throughout the second period of his production, we now briefly discuss these constitutive elements. Action is intended as a process which takes place within a social system made up of interdependent units; it can also set its boundaries. In other words, the system refers to a set of reciprocally oriented, non-randomly ordered and interdependent interactions among individuals, and to the conditions that make these interactions possible. In addition, the social system has analytically identifiable boundaries with other systems, e.g. those of personality and culture. A complex social system comprises several subsystems, or segments, each of which is functionally differentiated and identified by its own norms. Finally, a society is a collectivity and a community. It is not included in wider collectivities and communities and forms a "moral community" responsible for a plurality of functions. Considered from the point of view of its constant elements, the system is a stable structure. However, it does have a need to conform to its external environment (not only the physical environment, but also the cultural one, the latter being related to the personality of individuals) and hence is itself changeable. Therefore, the system has both a static and a dynamic aspect. It interacts with the aforementioned systems by giving to, and receiving from, each of them specific inputs and outputs. The need to conform to the environment may require some changes in the system structure. The concept of function connects the static and dynamic aspects of the system.

Parsons identifies four different essential functions, or "functional imperatives." Each of these imperatives corresponds to a particular subsystem of the social system. Through the "pattern-maintenance function," the values and individual commitment required for conforming to the normative patterns are preserved. Through the "goal-attainment function," the system is able to meet its needs, such as preserving its integrity in the face of changes to its environment. Through the "adaptation function," which makes it possible to obtain physical, cultural and economic facilities, the system obtains and distributes within itself what is necessary to achieve its goals. Finally, through the "integrative function," it maintains itself as a unit, its differentiation notwithstanding, in so far as it performs the integrative function. The latter takes up and assimilates the functional contributions provided by the subsystems. These functional imperatives concern the system, and are not an issue for single individuals. Analyzing the interactions among individuals therefore requires different explanatory categories.

The AGIL pattern allows for even minor changes to conceptual definitions. A case in point would be an action which carries a symbolic meaning (rather than a manifest behavior) where the pursuit of a goal is concerned. The AGIL pattern also makes it possible to distinguish among expressive, cognitive and evaluative actions. It may be applied at different levels of generality. Roles are stable interactive processes defined by rules. Their stability results from generalized norms, or values, and from specific norms for individual roles. A collectivity is a system of interactions the elements of which share a normative culture. It is this that distinguishes them from others. A single individual therefore can participate in several collectivities. Social equilibrium can be analyzed as a dynamic process, in so far as one shows how change results from a relation between the system and its environment, the relation between the two being reciprocal, i.e. the environment is, in turn, modified by the social system. This process assumes that contributions external to the social system are utilized. These resources are also employed by any one of the subsystems as resources for its own functioning.

Norms and values, which belong to the cultural system, are an example of resources which are external to the social system. Other necessary resources come from the personality (conceived as a system) of individuals and from their organisms. By contrast to this, the system's ability to maintain its own structure as well as its values and legitimacy orientation is a real resource and internal to the system. The systems that are hierarchically placed (in Parsons' own words) at the top in terms of information, but at the bottom in terms of energy (i.e. their ability to contribute to other systems), regulate the flow of interactive transactions between the social system and other systems. This flow makes use of circulation and interchange media, all of which have symbolic significance. They relate phenomena which are different but relevant to the human condition and place them in particular a system or subsystem. For example, the social system is set in relation to the cultural system, or within the social system, the political subsystem G is set in relation to the economic subsystem A.

The system needs to have available generalized media of interchange. This results from differentiation of its social structures since they make use of these media as mechanisms of integration. At the level of the social system, circulating and interchange media consist in:

1. Money, as an instrument of the economic subsystem, which allows for market functioning and development. It creates resources/facilities which are then mobilized for performing economic functions.
2. Political power, as an instrument of the political subsystem. It allows for the mobilization and use of the resources.
3. Prestige, or influence, as an instrument situated in the integrative system. It makes it possible to elicit a generalized commitment to solidarity values. Finally,
4. Pattern preservation, as an instrument, situated in the L subsystem (pattern maintenance) and assigned to the function of preserving the social system through a commitment to enforcing norms and values. Norms are binding obligations, and values are conception of what is desirable.

At the level of the action system, which is more general than that of the social system, circulation and exchange media consist of:

1. Intelligence, as an instrument situated in the A organism system. It is through this that resources for the solution of cognitive problems can be mobilized.
2. Performance ability, as an instrument situated in the G personality system. This aims at the achievement of systemic goals by making use of the cognitive, affective and moral means which the subjects have at their disposal.
3. Affection, as an instrument situated in the I system. This aims at integrating the action system by permanently binding some individuals to others and to the collectivities to which they belong. It thereby allows for the establishment of a moral order.

4. Definition of the situation, as an instrument situated in the L system. The
function of this is to establish the interchanges and the boundaries of the
AGIL systems, which in turn form the larger action system.

Within the control mechanisms of the social system there is a hierarchy
of generalities, and consequently, of use possibilities. Money is placed at the
highest level of generality, and so has the greatest possibilities for circulating
within this system. This is followed by power (especially political power),
influence and, finally, commitment to the enforcement of cultural values. The
institutions in the context of which monetary transactions are carried out, are
property rights, job organization and contract. Parsons dwells in particular
on the political system and on influence. These will be therefore be given
close consideration here. Political power is institutionalized in the form of
authority. Together with power in general, money and influence, authority
has coercive power and it is exercised by those who exert it. However, it is
distinguished from coercive power by the fact that it possesses it is institutional legitimacy and it can to make effective decisions that are not binding
on those who are subject to a given political authority. Power is not therefore,
intrinsically effective. It is rather a symbolic medium for enforcing commitments or obligations to collective action. It legitimates authority, social
solidarity, and integration.

Like money, political power can be invested, in the sense the holder of
power can make legitimate decisions which have long-term consequences
for him or herself and for others. The exercise of political power is not, to
borrow the game theory language that Parsons here employs, "a zero-sum
game." That is, the benefits which accrue for some persons do not necessarily result in a corresponding disadvantage for others. The power holder can,
indeed, make decisions that are binding on others without being obliged to be
immediately responsible for them, and without having previously received a
specific mandate. Hence benefit can potentially accrue to all. Obligating the
holder of power holder to keep particular engagements would mean with-
drawing trust and would no longer allow power to function as a medium of
circulation and interchange. The legitimate exercise of power reduces the use
of coercion to n exceptional measure. A case in point would be when there is
no longer trust in the credit system and investors ask the banks to have refund
their deposits.

Likewise, monetary investments are based on generalized trust, on the assumption they can be used as symbolic circulation and interchange media, since
the gold reserve of a State is not sufficient to guarantee that money performs
this function. Effective analogies can be drawn between money and power as
regards their functions. Influence should not be mistaken for power and wealth.

These may all be generalized circulation media, but influence, in so far as it is distinct from power and wealth, assumes an intention to affect others' attitudes and opinions through persuasion. Those who avail themselves of their power to influence others, offer them benefits, refrain from any form of coercion towards them, and do not appeal to norms and rules to obtain their commitment. Persuasion therefore involves a relation based on assumed solidarity between the parties; it also presumes a collective identity that includes both of them. Solidarity is generalized to a plurality of subsystems, for an actor, be it an individual or a collectivity, often belongs to more than one group.

There are also different kinds of influence: Political influence is a generalized means of persuading others as regards their political decisions. There is also influence based on trust. It is important if system resources are to be distributed properly and if at least some of the concerned persons cannot exert control over this distribution. Still another form of influence appeals to a generalized commitment to loyalty in which those who are trusted commit themselves to behaving correctly in a wide range of non-rigidly defined and pre-established circumstances. Finally, a particular kind of trust is granted to those who interpret legal norms (judges, lawyers) and religious norms (priests), or scientific knowledge (e.g. doctors). This kind of influence assumes their adherence to norms or notions, as well as their commitment to put them into practice. Such a commitment is a solidarity factor placed near the top of the hierarchy of the elements that control the action system. Parsons examines this theme in depth in an essay entitled *On the Concept of Value-Commitments* (Parsons 1969: 439–472).

Written in 1968, this essay belongs to the subsequent period of Parsons' production. But he himself underlines the continuity between value-commitments as generalized circulating and interchange media, and the other media he had already considered, in particular, money. Value-commitments are a generalized medium aimed at putting into action some obligations that are morally binding for those who share a given set of values. These commitments are partial, in the sense that they involve a particular level and kind of enforcement and responsibility. A complex action system, as that which results from social differentiation, can be guided and integrated or coordinated only by a differentiated and flexible system of values. It assumes a generalized commitment to enforcement, and therefore widespread loyalty to these values. By contrast to this, a rigid and non-differentiated system of values, as can be found in societies dominated by fundamentalist ideologies and religions, would involve the reverse, namely, a process of social conformism or de-differentiation.

Parsons identifies some of the general conditions of equilibrium in the social system and in the other action systems: a) The *inertia principle*: The process of an action continues its course as long as it is not disabled or diverted by opposite motivational forces. b) The *action and reaction principle*: In an action system, every change of direction in a process is balanced by an equal and opposite change in motivational force. c) The *effort principle*: Every rate of change in an action process is directly proportional to the amount of motivational force that has either been used or withdrawn. d) The *principle of systemic integration*: Each pattern in an action system either remains in its position within the system, or is removed from it, depending on its contribution to the equilibrium and the integration of the system.

Processes, which maintain a systemic equilibrium in social systems, control deviant tendencies, be they individual or collective, through the application of a variety of positive and negative sanctions. In contrast to this, structural change involves breaking the boundaries of the social system or its subsystems. This break may result from endogenous strains. These can be found within personalities or culture. There are therefore located inside the system of norms, or even inside the social system itself, as when obligations inherent to the roles connoting a kinship system do not accord with those resulting from occupational roles. Systemic boundaries may also be broken as a result of forces exogenous to the social system. A case in point would be the social innovation brought about by a charismatic leader (assuming that this change could not be ascribed to a previously existing system of values).

Over time, a system moves from one condition, or phase, to another. Each phase is defined by a particular combination of alternatives as is observable from its pattern variables. The transition from one phase to the next is, to a great extent, regulated and controlled by institutionalized social norms. These make it clear how each member should behave and establish the sanctions (i.e., rewards and punishments) that can expected in return for certain behaviors. Norms are system properties, not the property of individual actors. Their primary function is to keep the phases of systemic change in harmony with one another and with the system as a whole. These phases, four in all, are defined by the functional activities that take place in each of them and by the society's orientation toward its objects, be they persons or things. According to Parsons, systems reveal a general tendency to move from an adaptive phase A, or from an integrative one I, to a phase G (in which the system orients itself to the pursuit of its goals), and to a phase L (in which motivations and personal commitment are preserved or used in the systemic action). Phases G and L designate movement in different directions. These are independent of one another yet interdependent. In both cases, motivational energy flows through the system.

The term *motivational energy* defines an impulse, or "urge" on the part of the actor. He makes this available to the social system in so far as he uses this energy. A system is not in a condition of equilibrium, and is therefore stressed, if this energy is used in ways that are non-functional. The system, as constituted by actions and things and represented by the four functional AGIL quadrants, in turn defines a macrocosm of events. The constitutive parts of this macrocosm, for example the quadrant I (integrative function), in turn, form a microcosm which is regulated by specific norms. This microcosm can be further subdivided into A, G, I, and L quadrants, each also designating symbolic processes of interpersonal communication as regulated by specific norms. Phase I (latency) indicates, in this case, the condition of the subsystem before and after interaction has taken place. It does not therefore connote the interaction itself.

Motivational energy makes it possible for the microcosm to undergo a transition from one condition to another, i.e., input received in the form of information or commitments, and the output given in the form of facilities and achievements, ensure this. Processes of individual and systemic learning and change take place within an action system. The latter vary in relation to the values of the social system, its purposes, its developmental phase or condition, and its (cognitive, *cathectic* or evaluative) relation to its internal or external objects. These processes select and define the purposes of the units that constitute the system, and they bring about integration among them in accord with the functional requirements of the system. The system's structural differentiation process produce differentiated roles and specific purposes for individuals, and, for its subsystems, functional specialization and specific values within a common system of values. An instance of this would be the subsystem of occupational roles.

THE MARSHALL LECTURES AND ECONOMY AND SOCIETY

Two other works dealing with the convergence of economic and sociological theory belong to this period as well. In the first, the so-called *Marshall Lectures* (1953), Parsons formulates analytical categories and outlines his thinking on the economy as a social system, a system which therefore has non-economic aspects. The second work, written with Neil J. Smelser and entitled *Economy and Society,* dates to 1956 and deals in particular with the institutional structure and change of the economy. We briefly summarize both works here. They are marked by conceptual and theoretical continuity with *The Social System* and *Working Papers in the Theory of Action.*

The *Marshall Lectures* includes some lectures given by Parsons at Cambridge in 1953 to an audience of economists. Parsons had received a university education in economics and in this cycle of lectures aimed to analyze economy as a particular subsystem of the social system (indicated here by the letter A). Its specific function is to make scarce resources obtained from the external environment available to the system, and so to provide other system units and consumers with the goods and services they need (hence the term *adaptive function*). The goods and services supplied by the subsystem flow to the other subsystems and to the social system as a whole in exchange for money. This is governed by: 1) Mutual, institutionalized expectations as they are regulated through property and contractual rights, 2) The economic values prevailing in the economic system (especially, those relating to the values of production efficiency and property), and 3) Individual and organizational motivations for correctly and carefully performing their economic roles. Non-economic factors, such as family and work ties, may limit the effectiveness of the usual mechanisms for re-balancing the market, e.g. supply and demand, prices and competition. Therefore, economic and sociological theorists may find it convenient to the advancement of their sciences to formulate a common conceptual and theoretical scheme.

These themes are resumed and further developed first in *Economy and Society*, but to a still greater degree so in subsequent works (see in particular, Parsons 1978: 435–440). Bearing in mind the functional division into four parts (designated by the acronym AGIL), Parsons aims at formulating a widely applicable conceptual scheme, or "paradigm" (Bourricaud 1981: 133–134). This paradigm can disclose the constitutive elements, or subsystems, of the general action system, and the relations among them. In *Economy and Society*, Parsons attempts to relate economic theory to the sociological theory, the latter being identified with the theory of social systems. He considers economy to be a subsystem of the social system, functionally separate from other subsystems, and (functionally) differentiated into the sectors, or subsystems, A, G, I. and L. Each of the four subsystems of the component A (the economic subsystem) has, institutionally regulated contiguity, interchange and integration relations with the four subsystems that make up each of the other components of the social system (G, I, L). For example, the goal-attainment function of the economic system relates to the parallel function on the subsystem L (pattern-maintenance) because monetary exchanges are used not only to obtain goods and services, but also as a symbolic means of achieving prestige (for an in-depth examination of the AGIL pattern in *Economy and Society*, see Holton 1986: 49–90).

Furthermore, the economic subsystem A receives from the political subsystem G the capital necessary for supporting its production capacity, and so is better equipped also for attaining the goals of the social system as a whole. As Parsons and Smelser argue, the other subsystems relate to one another in a similar fashion. Accordingly, the whole range of subsystems can constitute an integrated social system. When the processes of change to the economic system are not brought about by causes internal to the system, they result from a change which has occurred in the relations between that system and others. However, the ultimate cause is a change in the system of values, and consequently, in the institutional structure. Economic theory should therefore be considered a particular case of the general theory of action. It is only by taking this theoretical assumption into account that we can analyze economy as a subsystem of the social system, one which relates to all the other subsystems by both providing and receiving input and output.

CONCLUDING REMARKS

In the second period of his production, Parsons completely revised his conceptual apparatus in several ways. He shifted his focus from the concepts of norm, institution and social system, made a distinction between this system and the cultural and personality systems, and classified five sets of alternative orientations for actors (*pattern variables*), i.e. their possible orientations toward the roles they perform within the social system. These alternatives, or dilemmas, are used to analytically define the prevailing value orientations in a social system and to identify different kinds of social structures, in particular, the industrial one. According to Parsons, this social structure is the only one compatible with capitalism. It is characterized by universalism, specificity, affective neutrality and achievement-orientation. The prevalence of one or another value orientation in a social structure requires appropriate role performance and correct enforcement of norms. These, in turn, assume that actors are socialized in such a way as to learn norms and values, and are therefore in a position to control personal deviant tendencies.

The processes which unfold in the individual personality must be reconciled with social system requirements. As noted, deviance produces strains that can endanger the system stability if appropriate social control mechanisms are not put into effect. The conceptual scheme described with the acronym AGIL, formulated some years after the pattern-variables frame, identifies the functional systems that taken together, make up the general action system, and defines the relations among these systems. The general action system, and the systems that constitute it, tend toward a condition of equilibrium if strains or other endogenous or exogenous causes of change do not interfere. Specific functional imperatives (attainment of facilities, the achievement of goals, and pattern maintenance and integration) correspond to each system.

The social system receives from the cultural system resources/facilities, such as beliefs and institutionalized values. Other resources come from the personality of individuals and from their organisms. Systems, as designated by the acronym AGIL, are hierarchically ranged in the order of decreasing access to information and increasing use of energy (Parsons here uses the term *cybernetic hierarchy*). Generalized symbolic media of interchange connect them. For the social system, these media consist in: money, political power, prestige and influence, and a commitment to maintain norms and values. The AGIL conceptual pattern can be applied in analyzing both the generalized action system and the systems (or subsystems) that constitute it. Parsons and Smelser considered the economic system to be a functionally differentiated subsystem of the social system and discussed it at length.

Chapter Four

The Third Period (1964–1979)

PRELIMINARY REMARKS

In the third and last period of his production, the end of which coincided with the end of his life, Parsons continued to keep to the conception of action system, the original formulation of which dates back to the first period (action frame of reference). He also continued to use the concept of the social system, the AGIL scheme, and the generalized interchange media classification. All of these belong to the second period. However, now for the first time, he began to study the problem of social change in depth. To do this, he introduced the key concepts of evolution, differentiation and adaptive upgrading. In the meantime, he also began to deal with the theme of the relations among the three aforementioned systems (the social, the cultural. and the personality systems) and the specific biological processes of the living systems, as well as those related to the physical environment (Parsons 1964b; 1966; 1971; 1977: 279–320).

The last part of this period is characterized by the formulation of a complex conceptual quadripartition. Here, the AGIL scheme is taken up once again, but radically revised as he sought to take into account other systems in addition to the action systems (the social, the cultural, and the personality systems). This new quadripartite pattern conceptually frames the human condition as a "telic" system. That is to say, it attempts to address human beings' search for an ultimate meaning by discovering one which can provide a foundation and give order to their own empirical and cognitive world. In a cybernetic information and control order, the telic system is assigned the highest rank because it gives significance and orientation to human action (Parsons 1978: 352–433; 2007: 428–429). In what follows, we shall first examine the theme of evolutionary change, and then that of the human condition.

EVOLUTION AND DIFFERENTIATION

Evolution concerns change to a system, for example the social system, when this change is produced by the environments to which the system relates. Differentiation is the process by which a functionally and structurally well-established unit of a system, or a subsystem, splits up into two or more units. These are distinct from each other and from the previous unit. It is then possible to distinguish among different stages, or steps, in the process of evolutionary change of a system. This is done through differentiation and adaptive upgrading in relation to the environments in which the system is situated. Concerning the social and the cultural systems in particular, each stage distinguishes itself from the previous ones by a decisive change in the normative structures. On these grounds, Parsons thinks it is possible to identify a primitive, an intermediate and a modern stage of systemic development.

The transition from the primitive stage to the intermediate one is characterized by the introduction of written language. In fact, this innovation, has allowed for the immense spread, over time and space, of a symbolic culture which is autonomous in relation to specific social contexts and has stabilized many social relations. In addition, it has allowed for critical analysis of written documents and made possible the introduction of innovations in the form of new documents and new interpretations thereof. The cultural systems of the societies of Ancient Greece and Israel formed the "seedbed societies" for the cultural innovations that occurred in several other societies. They therefore had decisive importance for the evolutionary process. The transition from the intermediate stage to the modern one has, by contrast, been marked by the establishment of a codified normative system, and, so also, a legal system. Generally speaking, progress in the evolutionary process has depended on increased social differentiation. In fact, this differentiation process has made it possible for the cultural factors, which are at the top of the control and information cybernetic hierarchy, to be freed from physical and organic constraints. The latter are to be found at the bottom of this hierarchy, but at the top of a hierarchy of conditioning factors.

From the process of differentiation there results a problem of integration, that is to say, a problem of functional coordination among these units. Adaptive upgrading is the process through which a system, in particular, a social system, receives either from the outside, or from its internal components, facilities that liberate it from previous restrictions. These allow it to better conform to its (physical, organic, cultural) environments without being subject to too many strains. Therefore, the system can be better integrated, and consequently, better attain its goals and perform its primary functions. These external facilities can be of a different nature. The cultural system, especially the Catholic and Protestant religions and Roman law, yielded new differentiation and legitimation opportunities for the social system, and consequently, new opportunities for inclusion and integration. This is the result of a process of value generalization. From the changes that have occurred in a democratic fashion in the political system, and from the separation between church and state, new opportunities for inclusion have resulted in a system of citizenship. The processes of functional and structural differentiation and adaptive upgrading produce a social system that is more complex than the previous one because they include in their constitutive units a greater number of goals and functions.

When differentiation occurs and adaptive upgrading processes unfold, strains can develop between the social, the cultural and the personality systems. If system integration is to proceed, then a general system of values is necessary. It must be capable of legitimating this greater variety of goals and functions, and allowing for the formation of a moral community. Evolutionary change is also defined by an inclusion process, one which stands in contrast to differentiation in the sense that elements which are peripheral to the system, become included in it and integrated with the other constitutive elements. Inclusion, which can either follow or precede a differentiation process, can contribute to the creation of a moral social community. This happens, for example, when different religious groups take on an ecumenical cast, and thereby de-emphasize their differences.

A societal community, i.e., a complex network of collectivities intertwining with defined loyalties, is the outcome of a successfully completed process of differentiation and evolution. It is connoted by members' widespread and long-lasting solidarity. In a cybernetic control hierarchy, a societal community is placed at the highest level. In fact, it is particularly rich in information that can be transferred to all its members because there are communication opportunities among them that cannot be found at lower stages of cultural and social development. A written language is also available at less advanced stages, but the bonds of solidarity that link the members of a societal community and transcend social and cultural differences can be found only at this stage of evolutionary development. A generalized and institutionalized system of values provides normative order and legitimation to society as a whole, even when it is differentiated into a variety of constitutive elements. Alternative non-ascriptive socialization and loyalty sources in relation to the kinship system, which is itself ascriptive, as well as religious sources of legitimation and integration, are requisite for the processes of differentiation and evolutionary change.

A break with parental authority and religious legitimation makes it possible for individuals to belong to several collectivities simultaneously.

They can demonstrate loyalty to all of them. Another consequence of such a break is the multiplication of social roles and of sources of prestige and influence. Still further differentiations occurs as a result of the individual cultural development that flows from this double break from family and religious traditions and the emancipation from specific territorial limits. From a political-legal point of view, new civil, political (i.e. democratic associations and organizations), and social (i.e. pertaining to a welfare state) rights are granted and protected thanks to the fact that legal systems develop independently of political institutions. This opens the way to more effective forms of political organization, and, consequently, to greater social integration. In the political-administrative area, bureaucratic organizations whose aim is to guard the public interest also become established; in the social area, nonprofit organizations and professional associations. Likewise, the expansion of primary and secondary education makes it possible to approximate the goal of equality for all, equality understood from a political point of view and also in terms of economic opportunities. The importance of inherited privileges is thereby reduced, and modern societies become possible by changes of decisive importance, changes which Parsons calls "revolutions." These occurr in the economic (industrial revolution), political (democratic revolution), and educational (educational revolution) arenas.

Finally, from an economic point of view, the changes which take place in the economic subsystem and have been made possible by the development of the monetary economy ensuing from the industrial revolution, involve the development of the market system. Thus the standard of living is improved, and new and more efficient production technologies are introduced thereby meeting the needs of masses of consumers. In fact, production is more efficient in a factory than within a domestic community. The latter, since it is no longer burdened by a productive function, can better perform other integrative functions pertaining to it, such as socialization.

The economic subsystem is linked to the other subsystems of the social system by symbolic and generalized interchange media. As noted, these media are institutionalized. They circulate during transactions and are convertible into each other. However, they can mediate only certain kinds of interchange and their overall availability is not pre-determined. The process of value generalization plays a key role in social evolution. Without this process, it is neither possible to achieve stability nor to bring about any evolutionary upgrading in the social system, and so also in the human condition. The latter can be conceptualized in different terms compared to the AGIL pattern of the aforementioned social, cultural and personality systems. The reference to the human condition involves, in fact, the inclusion of new categories, even if they are functionally classified within the quadripartite AGIL scheme.

These categories must be understood in the increasing *cybernetic* order of information and control, and in the decreasing order of *energy* and conditioning factors:

A. The "physical-chemical" system is placed at the sub-organic level. Though it is external to the human condition and thus does not possess symbolic information, it is an ultimate source of *energy*. It provides the necessary facilities for the survival of all living systems.

G. The "human organic system," which is also external to the human condition is oriented toward the functioning of the organism, i.e. it seeks to maintain the conditions of the physical-chemical system and the relations of functional interdependence with the action system. The "telic" system establishes the significance of organic life for the human condition.

I. The "action system" is to be understood as part of the human condition. It is continuously subject to conditions of interchange with the other systems, and for any human being, it performs an integrative function (human organism and personality). Considered form a temporal perspective, the *action system* involves *instrumental* processes. It is through these that facilities are developed for future use; it also involves "consummatory" processes, through which such facilities are used and destroyed.

L. The "telic" system, which is intrinsic to the human condition, is oriented toward searching for the ultimate meaning of the world. It is rich in information about the problems of suffering and evil. It is a "latent" system, and, consequently, one which does not directly reveal itself through actions. Instead, it goes beyond them and confers on them an "ultimate" meaning (Holton 2001: 156–157; for an introduction, see Bourricaud 1981: 189–231).

AMERICAN SOCIETY

Lastly, we wish to discuss a posthumous work by Parsons, published under the title *American Society. A Theory of the Societal Community* (Parsons 2007). This work, which Parsons could not bring to completion, was edited by Giuseppe Sciortino. In his preface, Sciortino mentions its classification in the Harvard University archives. He also outlines the editorial standards he has followed. Although it could not be completed before Parsons' death, the thinking it contains had reached a very advanced stage at that time. It reviews some previously formulated theses and concepts. As Sciortino points out in the introduction to the chapter dealing with the theme of ethnicity, it provided an overview of some previously published writings (Parsons 2007: 309). Compared to earlier works, it can be considered an extension and an in-depth examination of certain themes: the constitutive elements of societal community; the conceptual and theoretical relation between social class and the labor market, the employment system and the professions; community and society in the United States, with particular reference to class and ethnic differentiation; and, lastly, political and communication processes and institutionalized individualism.

Parsons defines the societal community as a functional subsystem which oversees the problems associated with integration of problems of society as a whole (Parsons 2007: 22–23, 54–55). In his introduction to this work, he states that the societal community is the theoretical object of study, in particular to the integrative problems in the American society (Parsons 2007: 23). These problems are evidenced in, and were simultaneously produced by, several of the crisis situations that occurred in the United States during the 1970s. Parsons focuses on the events that led to President Nixon's resignation, stressing his deliberately misleading strategies, e.g., the abusive appeal to national security interests and the resort to secretiveness. Nixon and his collaborators attempted to remain in power by implementing these strategies. But, instead, they created a climate of suspicion and distrust. Another example of a crisis in the integration of American society has its origin in the university system.

The educational revolution, which took place in the 1960s and 1970s, because of the marked increase in student admissions, gave rise to intense competition for access to the most prestigious universities. The selection process rewarded a rational and cognitive orientation to education rather than meeting students' requests to study subjects which they considered worth pursuing, even at the cost of disregarding the acquisition of essential knowledge. Thus the widespread expectations for a truly effective upgrade to educational qualifications were not fulfilled. This caused frustration and tension among the students, because the universities continued to adopt selective admission and evaluation procedures based on cognitive standards of rationality rather than on ideological criteria. Students and some progressive teachers were claiming the latter were most important If such standards had proved successful, the necessary distinction between the disinterested search for objectively valid knowledge, on the one hand, and political and social commitment, on the other, would have failed. Knowledge itself would have undergone a considerable process of redefinition and simplification. Students' protest led the university authorities to award some grants to those who endorsed this ideology, but, as Parsons argues, this did not lower the professional competence levels of the academic staff.

The next chapter is essentially theoretical and deals with societal community in relation to its internal and external environments. Societal community is a social system property. It performs an integrative function (quadrant I of the social system) and relates to economy (quadrant A), to institutions of political government (quadrant G) and to the fiduciary system (quadrant L). The integrative function involves solidarity maintenance mechanisms for the entire social system, and therefore, controls any propensity to harm or destroy individuals and collectivities belonging to this system. It is possible to perform the integrative function if the members of a collectivity recognize common norms and values. Norms connect the functionally differentiated subsystems of the social system, whereas values provide a reference system shared by all subsystems.

In addition to the values that prevail in American society, solidarity factors include: first, the commitment of individuals and collectivities to positively evaluated associations; secondly, decisions which are binding for the societal community because they are accepted insofar as they are legal; finally, distributive justice criterion which conforms even implicitly, to consensus as to what constitutes the collective interest. Individuals, insofar as they perform social roles, and collectivities, are constitutive elements of a social system. They relate to one another both because individuals can be members of the same collectivity, and also because individuals and collectivities can share a common normative order. In other respects, however, these constitutive elements are differently characterized. In fact, individuals differ from each other not only in terms of roles, but also in other ways (according to age, sexual gender, residence, etc.). Furthermore, they can perform several roles, and may therefore belong to several collectivities at the same time. In addition, they are frequently subject to different normative orders, for the normative system is differentiated.

The constitutive elements of a social system, i.e. individuals and collectivities, do not necessarily belong to a single normative order. How it is then possible to provide solidarity to a societal community? Parsons argues that influence is not only a generalized medium of interchange (relevant in this case), but also a source of prestige, and therefore, integration. Since the normative order cannot find its source of legitimation within itself, this source should be sought in widely recognized normative structures even outside a particular normative order. This can happen if the social system is institutionally integrated: it is not a question of reconstructing an undifferentiated structure, such as a community, (Toennies) or a collectivity characterized by mechanical solidarity (Durkheim). In fact, the social system is functionally differentiated, and therefore capable of including new and different units which are themselves, in turn, differentiated.

The constitutive units of the social system (roles, norms, collectivities) instead, vary independently of each other and can interpenetrate each other.

Values are mainly part of the cultural system, while norms connect and pen- etrate both the social and the cultural systems. In the action system, order and solidarity result directly from these two systems, and not from the political or economic system. This order must continuously change if it is to conform to conditions external to the action system. Institutionalization, however, stabilizes it and allows for it to be being internalized by the individuals who participate in it. As regards American society, it consists of different ethnic groups, and is not actually a community, in Toennies' sense of the term. Its integration may result from the application of universalistic standards in- spired by a principle of cognitive rationality. The latter is intended to regulate the relations among its constitutive units. In that case, in Toennies' wording, non-functionally specific communitarian relations of solidarity based on af- fection accompany specific societal relations based on rationality.

To these theoretical considerations Parsons adds an historical excursus. He investigates the evolutionary potential of American society and stresses its innovative potential, the latter having been provided by Renaissance and the Protestant Reformation. In fact, a secular political and juridical thought inde- pendent of the Church succeeded in gaining ground during the Renaissance. The Reformation put an end to the separation of the secular and the spiritual spheres by asking each believer to live as a priest, in the absence of ecclesias- tical mediation. Furthermore, some radical tendencies within the Reformation weakened, or eliminated altogether, the hierarchical principle in favor of an egalitarian and collective organization. These innovations succeeded in de- veloping a large following in the United States due to the relative geographi- cal isolation of the American society. One feature of American society was that it granted early colonists immunity from religious persecutions. This laid the foundations for its subsequent evolutionary development.

According to Parsons, other factors also contributed to this process of evolutionary development: the limited importance of ethnic or religious minorities until the 19th century; religious freedom and tolerance toward dif- ferent faiths; the abolition of slavery after the Civil War and the lack of an agricultural proletariat in the North of the United States; the existence of an open frontier that allowed anyone to leave their parents' farm and make their own life elsewhere; the separation of powers (the legislative, executive and judicial powers); the secular nature of public institutions, and the existence of decentralized, democratic and constitutionally guaranteed political institu- tions. All this was accompanied, at a later stage, by market development, industrialization, and a considerable flux of immigrants from non-Anglo- Saxon countries. The "educational revolution" represented another important juncture in this process of change. The marked an ever-greater increase in Americans' school attendance has minimized the distinction between manual and non-manual labor, and diminished the pool of unskilled laborers available to the economy.

Moreover, the American higher education system has availed itself of an extensive network of colleges and universities, some of which, e.g. Harvard, are long established and prestigious. All of this has contributed to the development of professions and collegial, as opposed to bureaucratic associations. The strains that led to students' protests are surely evidence of a widespread state of discontent among the young population, but they are not unique to American society; similar riots have broken out in many other countries in which an "educational revolution" had taken place. However, American society has been exposed to external strains since World War I, because its political and military involvement has extended to the entire globe. Nonetheless, Parsons argues, these strains have not changed the basic liberal-progressive orientation of American society and its government. An imperialist and expansionist tendency has, indeed, always clashed with a lively internal opposition. The war in Vietnam is a case in point.

The third chapter, like the second, is theoretical in that it deals with values and other constitutive elements of the societal community. A value is here defined as a culturally patterned way in which one or more actors, placed in a situation or an environment, orient themselves to an object or a class of objects they consider desirable. Values vary depending on their level of generality. They constitute a system and show how actors relate to particular object. They are therefore not a property of individual actors or objects. Like any other element of the institutional structure, they have a normative reference that shows what can or cannot be desired. In addition, values have to be integrated in several respects with the other elements of the social system (roles, norms and collectivities). Should conflicts break out, whether visible or concealed, some integrative mechanisms have been provided for this purpose. Finally, values hold the highest position in the cybernetic hierarchy, and can therefore rule and control (but not determine) the other elements of the social system, and in general, of the action system.

Instrumental activism is the most important value for the American society, for it integrates the social and the cultural systems. This term refers to a predisposition to actively intervening in human life in order to reduce the distance between reality and ideality. It is a value is deeply rooted in the cultural and religious traditions of the United States. In fact, it has its origins in liberal Protestantism and the Enlightenment, and contributes to legitimating the equilibrium between the opposed tendencies of freedom and constraint, equality and inequality. In the societal community, which performs an integrative function, instrumental activism may produce strains and reduce solidarity in relation to the economic subsystem, because economic resources are unevenly distributed. Solidarity is an institutionalized value aimed at stabilizing positive affective relations among the elements of the social system. Solidarity within a subsystem can trigger antagonism toward other subsystems. Class struggles are a case in point, as are the actions of individual actors vis-à-vis some normative structure, since they change the sentiments and interests of others.

How then can the institutionalized value of individualism be harmonized with an appropriate level of solidarity? In other words, how can freedom be concordant with constraint? Parsons' answer to this centers on the concept of citizenship. Through the citizenship system, which includes civil, political and social rights, according to Marshall's typology, individuals (insofar as they are social actors) are integrated into the collectivities to which they belong. They therefore accept the norms and values of the differentiated societal community to which they are anchored. The value of equality ensures equal opportunity in principle through the welfare state. Solidarity is thereby institutionalized in the social community; at the same time, the equally institutionalized value of individualism can assert itself in the economic arena. The link between these two values is the legal system. The societal community (sector I of the social system) provides solidarity with itself and positively assesses that solidarity; it also receives solidarity from all the other sectors of the social system: from the fiduciary system L, in the form of commitment to positively evaluated associations, from political institutions G, in the form of collectively binding decisions, and from the economy A, in the form of claims made on scarce resources.

Certain limits result from the fact that a maximum of equality or freedom must be made compatible with the need for a minimum of stability on the part of the action system. One obstacle to equality arises from the difficulty of reconciling equality and inequality over the long term. There are generally accepted justifications of inequality. Quite often, these make use of functionalist arguments to legitimate inequality, and consequently to maintain long-lasting solidarity, from generation to generation. A case in point would be those based on age and sexual gender. The market legitimates inequalities produced by different levels of success among competing economic units. Likewise, the university system legitimates inequalities in terms of the different levels of influence and prestige that result from professional achievements in research and publications.

Regarding freedom, in the United States, constitutional norms establish the domain of legitimate freedoms. These are distinguished into freedom to pursue one's interests provided this does not prove detrimental to others, freedom to actively participate in decisions concerning one's life, and to create associations which represent such interests. Some individuals have a formally recognized right of participation and others do not. Equal opportunities are guaranteed to all by the Constitution without distinction of race, faith, or color of the skin. The values of equality (vs. inequality) and freedom (vs. constraint) orient the American system of values toward the individual. As mentioned, the societal community subsystem plays an integrative role in the American social system and takes institutionalized individualism to be a key value. In a societal community, these fundamental values, which, jointly considered, define *instrumental activism*, are classed into quadrant L, while market freedom is placed in the economic quadrant A, responsibility for collective interests, in the political quadrant G, and collective association in the integrative and fiduciary quadrant I.

Influence serves as an integrative mechanism in this community. It is defined as the ability to control access to information and to share it with others and thus fulfills an integrative function for the social system. A societal community is a community of peers with respect to equal rights, as is the case in a democratic State. Those who have influence in a societal community do not coerce, but rather persuade. In this way they can justify or contribute to a particular course of action. Effective use of influence depends on existing relations of trust between those who exert it and those who are subject to it. It can also create a relation of solidarity between them. The units, be they individuals or communities, that enjoy this right can have a varying capacity for inclusion, the maximum level of inclusion being the right of citizenship. The twofold assumption that participants are prepared to bear the costs of this, monetarily or otherwise, and to abide by its rules, applies in the case of a societal community.

Societal communities differ from one another not only in their capacity for inclusion, but also in their prestige, their functional importance within the wider social system to which they belong, their level of universalism (vs. particularism, i.e., the prevalence of cognitive rationality) and diffusion (vs. specificity, i.e., an individual's or a collectivity's degree of involvement in the solidarity-based group). The term *collective sentiment* defines the integrative mechanism acting at the general level of the social system. It also integrates the moral imperatives of this system with the typical moral imperatives of the cultural system, as well as the motivational imperatives of individual personalities. *Instrumental activism* designates a value that rewards those attitudes and behaviors which aim at controlling and mastering all the environments in which the actor or the collectivity are included.

Relevant environments are: the physical environment, which is provided with natural resources that can be exploited; the individual personality, which is an environment of the social system; society, which is an instrument for achieving other objectives, such as pursuing individuals' interests and freedoms; and the cultural environment, which is concerned, in particular, with the acquisition of cognitive resources. Through instrumental activism, an individual or a collectivity aim at understanding those sources that disturb the integration process. They also aim at achieving a satisfactory set of relations between the societal community and the other subsystems of the social system. (The fiduciary system is at the top of the cybernetic information hierarchy, and therefore at a higher level than the societal community; by contrast, political institutions and economy are assigned at lower levels). The autonomy of the integrative system I from the trust system L depends on the fact that an appropriate contribution provided by the latter. It takes the form of common values and justification of the bestowal of loyalty and commitment on positively evaluated associations. For example, in the case of the university, loyalty and commitment are valued insofar as they aid the institution in its pursuit of its cognitive goals.

These goals are compatible with the prevailing system of values, a system which justifies loyalty and commitment to the university in preference to other associations. Collective sentiments are a generalized symbolic media of interchange operative at the level of the general action system, whereas influence acts at the more specific level of the social system. Collective sentiments regulate the degree of legitimation degree, in terms of shared values, which a social system can receive from the cultural system when the former is viewed as an institutionalized order. Likewise, collective sentiments are the measure of the value of participation in different interactions and collectivities, including the societal community. They are also the symbolic place in which values are preserved. The intensity of collective sentiments and the degree to which they are made public provide a standard for evaluating solidarity within a social system. Collective sentiments contribute to creating and maintaining solidarity in social systems, that is, on the condition that these systems are stable and legitimated by the normative order, and that they form an affective (*cathectic*) object which can mobilize individual commitments.

The function of maintaining solidarity is also performed by intelligence, where intelligence is a cognitive medium made available to the action system for effectively distributing communitarian resources. The normative order of a community (in so far as it is based on solidarity), and the legitimation it enjoys, contribute to this as well in keeping with its typical system of values. Values and norms are not interdependent properties of the actor, but rather concern the relations between the actors themselves and their respective situation. Values are elements of the social system which have moral relevance; by contrast, norms have practical relevance for those who participate in an interaction. Internal coherence within the normative system is absolutely necessary to prevent conflict from developing in the social order and in the social system in general. The legal system is a system of written and customary norms based on values. However, if it is institutionalized, it becomes also a complex social organization, the court of justice being its main institution. It serves the primary function of establishing and regulating relations between those who carry out professional activities within the legal system and other actors.

Professionals make use of their professional knowledge to help non-experts legally define their situation and make decisions accordingly. The relation between these two categories, and in general between professionals and clients, is not only a cognitive one, but also a moral one. It is a relation of mutual solidarity, legitimized by the system of values in force in a given societal community. In modern differentiated societies, the legal system is the most important connection between the normative order and the structure of the interests of individuals and collectivities who form the constitutive units of society. The system of values is used to legitimize actions and commitments addressed to others, but not necessarily to create solidarity. The latter can also be found in criminal organizations. Parsons employs the word *justification* to describe the use of influence in making an evaluation and a choice in keeping with existing system of norms and values.

The use of moral standards to define situation and intelligence as solidarity factors aids in stabilizing a system of collective sentiments. Integration and solidarity in the societal community of the United States are hindered by problems associated with social classes and ethnic groups. Parsons dwells extensively on these two categories of social actors. As for social classes, processes of differentiation have occurred between corporate owners and managers, and in the employment system, between employees subject to authority and control, on the one hand, and professionals, on the other. Even if the latter are employed in an organization, they distinguish themselves from other employees by their higher education level and greater competence, and by the fiduciary responsibility assigned to them. Their importance for the organization of production in modern market societies has considerably increased.

A complex network of interchanges exists between economy and societal community, the result of which can be problems of allocative justice. As a matter of fact, resources are allocated disproportionately among individuals and among collectivities, in keeping with either openly expressed or concealed interests. They are also allocated in compliance with existing legal and social norms and with the system of values to which these interests are anchored. Legal norms, as institutionalized are made binding by the political system. Taken as a system, they perform an integrative function for the social system. To be effectively enforced they (especially those that regulate economic relations) require natural and economic resources/facilities. The fulfillment of the integrative function depends on the diffused (vs. specific) character of these norms; they are therefore are valid for a plurality of individuals. In other words, if they are to serve an integrative function, and consequently become a factor in the development of systemic solidarity, norms should be inclusive.

This implies that they are binding for individuals and collectivities, regardless of the particular (economic, social or ethnic) categories to which they belong. The solidarity that binds the members of these categories does not hinder the development of systemic solidarity, hence the need for a conceptual apparatus through which to analyze the different ways in which economic and non-economic elements combine in society and, particularly in the market. Normally, market transactions involve both economic interests and solidarity, the latter being non-economic in nature. Expressions like "trust," "commitment to valued associations," "and justification of claims to resources" refer to factors of solidarity. These institutionalize the conditions of market functioning and so make exchange possible.

Market regulation is carried out within in the framework of formal or informal contracts, but also through the normative regulation of private property. Thus legal limits have seen set as to what can be an object of transaction, and distinction has been drawn between ownership and corporate control. It is advisable that economic interests take into account a plurality of non-economic interests. By the same token, the latter can be mediated through different kinds of markets. The solidarity system involves the existence and integration of solidarity groups; these have differing capacities for inclusion and become interconnected with one another. In a situation in which consensus cannot easily be obtained, it is necessary to use influence to justify a course of action, e.g., a market transaction in which the parties have different and opposed interests. Though it may be temporary and limited in extent, the solidarity that can be achieved in a transaction contributes to the development of further, more extensive and long-lasting forms of solidarity. These establish themselves in the market and are, in turn, regulated by it. A case in point would be financial communities which assess the credit enjoyed by a firm that gets, or can get, capital on loan.

The labor market, considered as an institution, involves contractual relations between firms and employees, and, despite conflicts of interest, also assumes that contractually regulated relations are based on trust between the concerned parties. This relation aims at exchanging monetary remuneration for the advantages (or disadvantages) that result for the firm from an employment relation. It is governed by corporate bureaucracy, which avails itself of the services offered by professionals who have achieved specialized competencies and skills (in contrast to managers, of whom such competencies are not required). However, the provision of services has now become proportionally more important than the production of goods, a development that has accompanied the ever increasing levels of professional qualification achieved by many employees. A relation based on trust, out of which solidarity and social integration arise, assumes a mutual commitment on the part of both firm and employee. Each provides its counterpart with the goods and the services it needs.

Therefore, the labor market represents an important meeting point between the economic and non-economic aspects of the social system. In the United States, as in other industrialized countries, in their relations with their corporate counterparts, labor unions have enforced the practice of signing collective contracts. Such contracts regulate other non-economic areas of employees' life as well. As previously mentioned, today, the increasingly higher levels of professional qualifications acquired by a large part of the labor force have proved detrimental to those who do not have a higher education. At the same time, the number of professionals and managers has grown considerably. These employment categories are quite different from the category of the workers, as it was conceived by Marx and his followers. The labor market has become modified in a number of ways, e.g. differentiation of various types of employees, the ever-increasing number of professionals and managers, the importance of the organization or the prestige associated with a job. This process of redefinition has made it difficult to evaluate the labor market in ethical terms, and to offset the distributive inequalities that it causes.

In the subsequent chapter, Parsons deals with the theme of ethnic inequality. It has a cultural rather than an economic origin. In other words, in terms of Toennies' analytical categories, this form of inequality concerns the community (*Gemeinschaft*) rather than society (*Gesellschaft*). The word "ethnicity" is used here to distinguish a group with an historical identity and tradition of its own. "Ethnicity" began in Europe with the Protestant Reformation since it resulted in the creation of territorially defined ethnic communities. Each ethnic group is characterized by the same religion and language, and consequently by a common culture and by stable and widespread solidarity. A societal community is also an ethnic community, but the reverse is not always the case. In fact, the integrative function which a societal community performs does not necessarily include the social system. The United States is a societal community which has lost its original character of a white, Anglo-Saxon, Protestant ethnicity and become pluralist. It now leaves individuals free to choose whether, in which way, and to what extent they want to identify with their ethnic group of origin. This pluralism and the voluntaristic character of such group identification are not an obstacle to this ongoing identification.

Indeed, ethnic identity is often militantly claimed even when the assimilation process to the ruling culture has already taken place.

However, rather than leading to complete and active inclusion of all of the different ethnic groups in the American societal community, this process of assimilation may end in social disorganization, alienation, and anomy on the part of some groups (not only ethnic groups) which are intent on putting forward their own claims. In doing so, they do not care that they may undermine the solidarity and pluralism of the American society. In contrast to others, the Black (Afro-American) ethnic group has been defined not merely by a cultural but also biological characteristic, namely skin color. This has increased the difficulties associated with overcoming prejudice and exacerbated negative stereotypes. In some cases, it has also produced a reaction of extreme political-racial militancy (Parsons reminds us of the extremist organizations of the Black Panthers and the Black Muslims). Nevertheless, the Civil Rights Movement has promoted a strong upward mobility process for the black minority, for it has made it possible for some African-Americans to achieve high levels of power and hold prestigious positions.

On the other hand, ethnic diversity is not an exclusively American problem. It can be observed in other societies as well, both in developed countries and in those that have recently freed themselves from colonial domination. The *Gemeinschaft* complex includes widespread (non-specific) identification and solidarity relations among an unspecified number of individuals, ranging from a relatively narrow family group, such as a married couple with or without children, to an ethnic group with millions of members. The relations within an ethnic group are a case in point. By contrast, *Gesellschaft*-like relations, are specific, not based on solidarity, and characterized by cognitive rationality. The latter is a property of the social system, and not single actors. Diffuse *Gemeinschaft*-like relations and universalistic *Gesellschaft*-like relations, do not, however, create oppositions, because universalism is an attribute of external objects, in the sense that they are part of the actors' environment. On the contrary, specificity is a particular mode of orientation on the part of actors toward objects that are significant for them.

Gemeinschaft and *Gesellschaft* relations are not mutually exclusive; on the contrary, each subsystem includes both a *Gesellschaft*-like rational component and a *Gemeinschaft*-like normative one. Both types of relations can in general be found in an institution—for example, the secondary school or the market as well as in an action system. Organic and action systems, though they differ in many respects, share the same pattern of evolutionary change. Given that that the unit of analysis for social systems does not consist of individuals, but rather of roles, change occurs in both systems first in a protected environment, and later through increased differentiation and progress through various stages of complexity. In a social system, the protected environment is first the family, and then the school. Both are communitarian relation environments within the social system. For a society, the market is an internal, and consequently, protected environment; non-social environments, such as the cultural one, are external to it.

Evolutionary change involves an institutionalization process, a selective one through which, under favorable circumstances, cultural innovations can transform the internal elements of action systems such as symbolic systems and roles. These are elements of the action system, which first of all orient themselves to the actor's or others' organic system. If these elements are organized into consistent role patterns, or role sets, they cause the action system to be independent of the organic system. Historically speaking, the distinction between *Gemeinschaft* and *Gesellschaft* relations revealed itself during processes of structural differentiation. These processes coincided with the industrial revolution in England, on the one hand, and with the political revolutions in France, on the other. In the case of the former, the consequence was the formation of social classes, and in the latter, it was the formation of ethnic groups, the rise of nationalism, and the development of a relatively differentiated societal community.

In the United States, the differences among classes and ethnic groups have not involved a frontal opposition capable of endangering the integration process. This did, however, occur in Canada, between the English and French speaking populations. Because of the complex nature of American society and of all modern societies in general, there has been an intertwining of ethnic and class differences, and in general, an interpenetration of *Gemeinschaft* and *Gesellschaft* relations. Consider, for example, the frequently unclear boundaries and the interpenetration between work and leisure. Likewise, the action and the organic systems interpenetrate the family, the social system and the cultural system in religious and educational institutions. As regards the latter, the "educational revolution," i.e., the recent expansion of opportunities for education and of the "cognitive complex" in general, even to the upper educational levels, is yet another example of interpenetration between different systems.

In fact, within the wider action system, the cognitive system is part of the social system, the latter being regulated with respect to norms by the cultural system. Here reference is made to the relations between the quadrants I and L of the action system. In the even more general sector of the human condition, we find in modern society a fundamental continuity with the organic, action system and telic systems. Parsons argues this as follows: After the Protestant Reformation, the complex which he terms *instrumental activism* stimulated the development of relations between the complex of economic factors and that of moral factors (the latter also includes religious commitment). Both complexes of factors have developed in the direction of a single, differently integrated, action system. Within this action system, the structural differentiation process has produced a break in the dominance of moral-religious factors over personalities (in the action system, referring to the L-G quadrants). It has had repercussions on the integrative system and consequently, on the moral framework of the action system.

American Society continues with three fragments dealing with political and communication processes and institutionalized individualism. The first fragment closely examines the relations between societal community, on the one hand, and the economy and the fiduciary system, on the other. It then goes on to consider the constraints on these relations (Parsons 2007: 387). Particular reference is made to governmental institutions jointly considered (polity) and to the influence exerted over these institutions by private interests in competition with one another. Their regulation is mutual and takes place according to institutionalized standards. These demonstrate the legitimate limits to the exercise of moral freedom and influence. The generalized symbolic media of interchange between the subsystems of economy and societal community consist in money, which measures monetary costs and benefits from an economic point of view, and influence, which measures solidarity from the point of view of the societal community. The interchange media, which are assigned the function of maintaining solidarity and ensuring social integration between the fiduciary system and governmental institutions, are, respectively, moral integrity and solidarity. Finally, the interchange media between societal community and the institutions of government are, respectively, influence and power.

Transactions carried out within the societal community imply that processes are in place for disseminating information. These not only avail themselves of the press, but, since 19th century, they have employed technologies that make mass communication possible through the so-called mass media (newspapers, radio and television). The moral aspect of communication is important to these media in two respects. First, because they can take a stance on matters of social and public morality. Some influential newspapers, for example, played a leading role in promoting President Nixon's resignation and continue to influence public opinion on controversial ethical issues. But the moral aspect is relevant to mass media for another reason as well. They contribute to the definition of legitimate boundaries for the exercise of influence in relation to prestige, on the one hand, and to the other interchange media (money, power, commitment to values), on the other. It is through the latter that the societal community is set in relation to the other functional subsystems of the social system.

While the general action system includes the social system along with the cultural, personality and behavior (or organism) systems, it is the cultural system that provides the social system with the necessary moral standards for building a social order. The personality system provides it with integration factors, such as attachment (or *cathexis*) to social roles and identification with them. Finally, the organism system provides it with impulses to action and to the capacity for situational understanding. These impulses are necessary to give significance to affective elements and rationally order them so that they can be learned by individuals. Only then can they contribute to the creation of a cognitive and moral order.

The integration of societal community with the other subsystems (culture, personality and the behavior) of the action system takes place through collective sentiments. These constitute a generalized interchange medium. Collective sentiments perform the function of combining the emotional aspect with the cognitive and evaluative-moral components of the action systems. All of these components are placed at different levels in the *cybernetic* information hierarchy. The evaluative-moral aspect is placed at a high level, subordinate only to the telic orientation. In other words, if it is to be satisfactory, the solution to a problem in the social system has to honor collective sentiment and conform to the legitimate interests of the elements that make up the social system (values, norms, roles, and collectivity). If collective sentiment can be recast into decisions to be made by governments place, then such an agreement can be put in place. And, such decisions are binding on all the members of a society.

The second fragment, a very short one, is a continuation of the first. It summarizes and examines in depth the theme of power. As Parsons argues, power, like money, is characterized by its ability to mobilize all useful or necessary resources to attain individual or collective goals. It is distinguished from money, however, in that it is legitimated by a position of authority. This position provides support to those who hold it, but cannot itself be legitimated by economic interests. Such authority, which rests on specialized knowledge, is exerted within a modern bureaucratic organization. Insofar as it minimizes the discretion of power holders it approaches the ideal type of this organization. But, there are two ways in which the exercise of power actually departs from this ideal type. First, if the power holder has achieved highly specialized knowledge; and secondly, if the members of an organization are not differentiate from each other in terms of power and so establish a community of peers marked by solidarity and based on the *Gemeinschaft* ideal in Toennies' sense of the term.

The third and last fragment of this work, which is also a very short one, deals with the theme of social stratification. Parsons first takes a stand against those of his interpreters who have considered him a status-quo supporter rather than a theorist and a student of conflict. He argues, in this connection, that in any society differentiated by social classes there are elements of both consensus and integration and that they extend across classes. There is therefore a false dichotomy at work here. The question of whether one element or another prevails can be only solved by the scholar's empirical research and evaluation. The processes by which the economy and the polity have been differentiated from societal community vary with respect to the industrial and the democratic revolutions. Understanding the nature and role of political interests requires that one study political organizations, since they pursue the goal of the collective good. Governments, in particular, aim at making and implementing decisions which are collectively binding.

Political interests, as expressed by those who participate in a system, are those which concern the effectiveness of mechanisms and processes that aim at achieving collective goals for which participants consider themselves responsible. Political interests always refer to power (in Parsons' sense of the term). They have collective purposes and an intrinsic tendency to expand, because they strive to control any uncertainty which could be a threat to their effective use of power. These interests are placed at a very high level in the *cybernetic* information hierarchy of a social organization, one which is even higher than that of economic interests. This explains why we resort to political actions to correct economic difficulties. Political interests, like economic ones, have a pluralistic character, since they are numerous and tend to counterbalance each other. There are, at present, no alliances between political and economic interests which are able to create power blocks sufficient to dominate the United States. American society is therefore not moving in the direction of a polarization between opposed political blocks, nor is it heading toward the social disintegration which would follow therefrom.

The final chapter of *American Society* deals with institutionalized individualism. It centers on American society and addresses the general theme of the balance between equality and inequality, freedom and constraint. The individual is here considered a complex entity, part of the action system and a unit of the social system. The individual is also an actor and an orientation subject both for other social actors and for himself. As an actor, the individual is included in a plurality of environments, the most external of which is the telic system. It is particularly relevant to the human condition. Problems of ultimate meaning, which orient the human condition and the action system, are conceptually located here. The actor's discretionary sphere is limited by the telic system; but at the same time, it enables the actor to interact in a conscious and responsible way with the environments in which he is placed.

Individualism developed initially in ancient Greece when the population was released from coercive political forces. It has unfolded further in context of Judaism and Christianity, and above all with the Protestant Reformation. Hallmarks of this process have been deliverance from the bonds of traditional culture, the development of a secular culture and, consequently, the possibility for individuals to freely choose the course of their own lives. Two opposite tendencies have revealed themselves in the philosophical field. On the one hand, Rousseau and Comte seek to level claims of individuality and negate their specificity by including individuals in a social collectivity. On the other, Utilitarians and liberals, in particular John Stuart Mill, claimed individual freedoms and rights. At the turn of the 20th century, Durkheim, Weber and Freud argued that action is not determined by instinct, and consequently, individual action is independent of biological heritage. People instead learn from childhood to interact with others and thus internalize discipline, and come to a consciousness of the normative and moral order of society. Through this socialization process, the personality and the social system become interpenetrated and thus share some constitutive elements.

The "cult of the individual," a problem tackled by Durkheim, is not a synonymous with egoistic interest, but instead points to the need to adhere to cognitive standards as guidelines for action and also to the need for a commitment to knowledge in service of affective, and therefore non-cognitive, interests and goals. According to Parsons, the major forms of action include both cognitive (i.e. rational) and non-cognitive (non-rational) elements. The problem of social order and its rationality can be better faced at an analytical level of the social system rather than at the more general level of the action system. On the other hand, as Durkheim argued in his dispute with Utilitarians, rationality is not the property of the individual. On the contrary, an action is rational when it conforms to the moral-normative order and so is anchored in the cultural and in the social systems.

In keeping with Parsons, the process of individuality development is part of an expressive revolution, one which is currently underway. It follows upon other historical processes, such as the industrial, educational and political revolutions, and has led to institutional individualism. This development has favored the individual ability to act in a responsible and autonomous manner; on the condition, however, that cognitive rationality and the moral-normative order are preserved. Both conditions are necessary to the social integration of modern differentiated societies because they counter intrinsic tendencies to anomy and social disintegration. Institutionalized individualism involves a synthesis of heterogeneous cultural elements. These can be used to overcome socio-cultural antitheses, such as that between capitalism and socialism.

CONCLUDING REMARKS

In the latter portion of his life, Parsons re-considered the AGIL conceptual pattern, but nevertheless extended its application to include the human condition.

The human physical-chemical and organic systems are placed outside it. By contrast to this, the action system, which includes the social, cultural and personality systems, and the telic system, which provides the empirical and cognitive world with ultimate meaning, and is placed at the top of a cybernetic information and control order. These are all now viewed as internal to the human condition. This effort to provide a conceptual framework for themes which Parsons considered sociologically relevant led him to focus not only on the human condition, but also on social change.

Evolution and structural differentiation are the analytical categories used to investigate social change. As compared to any previous stage of evolution, each later one is characterized by greater differentiation and further adaptive upgrading (of the social and cultural systems in particular) in respect to environment. It is on these theoretical-conceptual grounds that Parsons distinguishes a primitive, an intermediate and a modern stage of societal development. The transition from the earlier to the later stages was made possible first by the cultural systems ancient Greece and Israel and by their articulated symbolic complexes; it was then later further facilitated by the institution of codified legal systems. As the evolutionary process moves forward a system can better meet its goals and perform its functions. However, it also has to cope with growing problems of integration, and consequently, with inter-systemic strains. There is therefore the functional need for a general system of values through which an increasingly differentiated social system can be legitimated and strengthened, and the development of a moral and social community fostered.

The object of study of Parsons' last book, *American Society. A Theory of the Societal Community,* is integration in modern differentiated societies. According to him, the American society is the most outstanding example of a modern society thanks to its strong social and ethnic differentiation, the extensive development of the cognitive complex, its system of industrial relations, the expansion of professional jobs opportunities, and the regulation of the exercise of influence in the political system. This work reflects on some of the crises that arose in the political and educational system in the United States during the 1970s, and addresses the question of whether America can nonetheless consider itself a societal community, one in which *Gemeinschaft* and *Gesellschaft* relations combine. Parsons makes reference to the values of instrumental activism and individualism as they are institutionalized in the United States. These would cause strains on the social system if the American citizens were not integrated into a system of citizenship, and if the value of equality were not recognized as applying to all. The American people's inclusion in a common system of citizenship has prevented the development of conflicts between classes and ethnic groups. Parsons notes that the Civil Rights Law has succeeded in extending this inclusion to African-Americans.

Chapter Five

Research on Specific Themes

PRELIMINARY CONSIDERATIONS

In this chapter we deal with some inquiries carried out by Parsons between the 1940s and the 1970s. These works consist mostly in essays, some of which became famous and were reprinted several times. They focus on themes especially relating to the United States, and are concerned with the functioning of democratic political systems and the dangers to which they are susceptible (functional quadrant G of the social system). The social system, in turn, forms quadrant I of the general action system. The latter includes, in addition to the social system, also the cultural, the personality and the organism systems. Further themes addressed during this time period by Parsons are: economic and ethnic inequality in modern democratic societies and the consequences that inequality may have for social integration (functional quadrant I of the social system); finally, there are also the institutional factors of solidarity and socialization as these relate to educational and religious institutions (functional quadrant L of the social system) in particular. The functional quadrant A (economic institutions as a subsystem of the social system) is studied in detail in the monograph *Economy and Society* (1956).

These inquiries are empirical, that is, they deal with empirically observable phenomena. Parsons himself, however, refrained from personally carrying out such investigations as he preferred to draw on studies done by other researchers, and use them for his own theoretical purposes. In fact, he constantly strove to frame these inquiries in theoretical terms, making use of the AGIL conceptual pattern wherever possible, and relying on a structuralist-functionalist framework. Even though Parsons had not yet begun to use the AGIL pattern in the 1940s and early 1950s, in those years he wrote several remarkable essays on processes and institutions of the political systems of Germany

59

and the United States (see Gerhard 2002). In them he argued that democratic processes can undergo an authoritarian involution, and that the functioning of a society's political-parliamentary institutions can be hampered by internal divisions within the political system and/or by their insufficient coordination with others, especially the economic and cultural institutions. To supplement this functionalist explanation, Parsons considered the historical and social causes of these internal divisions and of this insufficient coordination. He also dwelt on the psychological and social mechanisms, i.e., the anxiety and tensions, or "strains," which may affect the stability and the functioning of political institutions in democratic societies. The German Weimar Republic and the United States Government were objects of his study.

ESSAYS ON POLITICAL SOCIOLOGY

We here briefly mention some of these works. A first essay, "Democracy and Social Structure in Pre-Nazi Germany" was published in 1942 (Parsons 1969: 65–81). It includes a comparative analysis of the effects of the industrialization and urbanization processes which were ongoing at the time in Germany and other industrialized countries, the United States in particular. Parsons seeks to understand how these processes impacted on the class structure and social-political culture up till the 1930s. He stresses the inconsistency of these outcomes in Germany. On the one hand, there existed a class structure that continued to hold to the conditions of a pre-industrial society insofar as the middle class accepted and sought to preserve the power and prestige of its aristocracy. This was evidenced in the prevalence of conservative or reactionary cultural ideals. On the other hand, there existed the typical economic system and institutional structure of a modern country. This inconsistency caused a good part of the German population to experience a condition of anxiety and psychological instability. Modernity was rejected by a large segment of the population as it was perceived to be extraneous to, and incompatible with, the country's traditions; also, romantic and anti-industrial tendencies came to the fore and were exploited by aggressive political movements such as Nazism.

The coeval essay "Some Sociological Aspects of the Fascist Movement," is thematically and temporally continuous with this earlier essay (Parsons 1969: 82–97). In this later essay, Parsons discusses the German condition of anomy and its various causes: the traumatic defeat suffered in World War I and the economic, social, and political instability that resulted from it; a system of values that was based on an exasperated nationalism, and was, to a large extent, hostile to capitalism; a weak social structure; and a deeply divided political system; one that had both a prevailing traditionalist component, and a minority component, the latter having been integrated into modernity. It was this anomic condition, rather than the hostility of capitalist interests, that was responsible for the widespread aversion to the institutional structure of the Weimar Republic and to what its fascist opponents took it to represent. In keeping with their views, German traditions had surrendered to the new liberal-democratic ideals as well as to socio-political forces introduced by the powers-that-be of the day.

Of the essays published in the 1950s concerning the American political system, we consider now two. They continue and further develop the thematic inquiry carried out in the previous ones. The first, published in 1955 with a postscript written in 1962 (Parsons 1969: 163–184), asks what made it possible for the extreme right movement, as led by Senator Joseph McCarthy, to garner a considerable political following and have a strong impact on the public opinion between the late 1940s and the early 1950s. In Parsons' view, the reasons for this can be found in the strains caused by the post-war international situation, particularly by the fact that the Soviet Union achieved the status of a world power. These strains overlapped with those caused by Great Depression of the 1930s. Costly governmental interventions in support of the economy followed in the case of the former. These interventions had been included in the New Deal, but clashed with the proud individualistic traditions of the American farmers. According to McCarthy's followers, who had mostly been recruited from this social stratum and from the lower-middle classes in general, the international communist challenge received a warm welcome from progressive intellectuals and garnered their support. Usually, they originated from a well-educated, privileged and urban milieu, and therefore, as McCarthy and his followers were convinced, were prepared to betray their country. In Parsons' opinion, the simplistic message behind his movement, one which did not distinguish at all between progressives and communists, led to a decline in trust in the institutions of democracy. It also demanded complete and exclusive political commitment in the name of patriotism and individualism. This deflation in political power, which is one of the generalized circulation media, is however, according to Parsons, incompatible with the complex and differentiated American political system.

The second essay considered in this chapter (Parsons 1969: 185–203) also concerns the American political system during the 1950s and 1960s. It consists in a review of the book by C. Wright Mills, *The Power Elites*, published in 1956. Mills argued that the United States had become an amorphous mass society, and the American citizens, the existence of democratic institutions notwithstanding, have, as a matter of fact, come to be governed by political, economic and military elites acting in concert. Parsons remarks that these assumptions can be countered by empirical and theoretical objections.

However, where these empirical objections are concerned, there is not only insufficient argumentation and documentation, but also the problem of the non-tenability of Mills' theses, according to which groups based on kinship, friendship, association and job ties have no social relevance. Parsons objects also to Mills' claim that government and parliament have become powerless in the face of economic interests; that, in the economic sphere, control of the big corporations is centered exclusively in the hands of owners, and does not also lie with managers. He also claimed that the power of the American military results from the international political circumstances of that period, and that it is subject to institutional control. This theoretical objection is reminiscent of a conception of political power as a generalized circulation medium. By conceiving power as a zero-sum game, Mills neglects to show how it is produced and which public interests it can serve.

Like the previous two essays, both of these demonstrate Parsons' concern with the stability of democratic-parliamentary systems and his search for the conditions that can make this possible. In addition, they have a common thesis: A complex, economically and socially differentiated society has a functional need for a democratic political system, one which is organized into a variety of political parties and based on a system of values. If there is to be generalized trust in institutions, this is the *sine qua non* of such systems. The theme of inequality was dealt with by Parsons on several occasions. We here refer, in particular, to his last essay, originally published in 1970. It is the most conceptually and theoretically elaborate of all of them. The functional quadrant I (integration) of the social system is, in this case, relevant to the theoretical and empirical emphasis Parsons places on the relation between social and ethnic inequality and social integration. The question he is asking here is this: how can inequality and integration be reconciled in a functionally differentiated society? Parsons explicitly restates Durkheim's questions about the kind of relation that exists between integrative norms and resource distribution, and about the way in which widespread solidarity is possible within differentiated societies (1977: 365; Parsons 1979: Chapter. 1).

His reply to these questions recalls the two-fold criteria that legitimate and justify inequality. On the one hand, political institutions can legitimate it provided they have sufficient power and authority to take decisions which are binding on others and serve collective goals and interests. On the other hand, when it is legitimated in general terms, inequality receives normative justification where diversity comes about in the context of equal opportunity, and where such diversity was supported by legal guarantees of freedoms, obligations and fundamental rights. In such cases, the prestige that is attached to a different institutionalized position (prestige being a generalized interchange medium) is indicative of this inequality. Differences in prestige are then justified by assigning different responsibilities and recognizing different competencies within a system of values. The value of integrity is shared across the social system, and public adherence to it requires widespread commitment to it, regardless of actors' occupational category. Integrity, along with competence, is a value of crucial importance in free professions; however, it is not limited to them. Professional integrity implies integration into the social system on the condition that it is a generally acknowledged and respected value. Thus, the social system forms a moral community in which trust is institutionalized.

Professions Sociology and Educational Revolution

In this work Parsons takes up once again his sociological treatment of the professions. He had formulated his views on this on several occasions during the second and the third periods of his production (1969, see Parsons 1978: 35–65). As he argues, in modern societies, the professions constitute a complex which performs specific functions involving the application of specialized knowledge, the transmission of these functions to subjects institutionally legitimized to receive them, and their continuous extension. The performance of these functions demands high levels of qualification and competence which can only be acquired through university education and are certified by diplomas and membership in professional associations. The professional association has a collegial, non-hierarchical organizational structure. Accordingly, it entails equal rights and obligations for its members, has norms governing formal membership, and values solidarity among colleagues.

The high standards of professional qualification and competence require that only professional colleagues, and not the general public (who are consumers of their services), are entitled to evaluate their services. Professionals do, therefore, individually and collectively exert their authority and power over their clients. The public uses their services on the assumption that they make appropriate use of their power, i.e. that they act on the behalf of the public itself, that the services they provide do derive from appropriate competence levels, and that these professionals adhere to the moral norms that regulate the professional-client relation. This trust has as its correlate professionals' responsibility towards the public, and consequently, their commitment to upholding the value of professional integrity. Individual professional reputations, and those of the profession as a whole, attest to this commitment. Relations between professionals and clients cannot therefore be defined merely in terms of the market; they are regulated by different norms.

The last work published by Parsons during his lifetime deals again with the sociological study of the professions. Co-authored with Gerald M. Platt, it focuses on the institution of the university, and refers in particular to the academic profession in the United States from World War II to the 1970s (Parsons, Platt 1975). Some other essays, which were also published in the last period of his production, are equally concerned with levels of higher education (Parsons 1978: 96–164). In these late essays, Parsons develops a thesis (one previously outlined), according to which the transition to modernity, which started in 17th century, was marked by certain processes of change. He considers these processes revolutionary because of the impact they have had on the human condition. These changes relate to the industrial and the democratic revolutions, and finally, to the educational revolution, i.e., that concerning higher education. They have brought about expanded possibilities for achieving goals and putting values into practice. Because of them, it has been possible to create new opportunities for both individuals and society, opportunities that conform to an organizational rule of conduct termed *institutionalized individualism*.

As previously noted, this term defines a cultural pattern, i.e., a pattern which makes it is desirable that solidarity flow from the equilibrium that develops between, on the one hand, the values of a pluralistic, differentiated society and individual freedom and dignity, and, on the other hand, the value of justice. The latter concerns individuals' and groups' possibilities for accessing positively evaluated goods and services. The American system of values also assumes the value of *instrumental activism*. This assumes an active attitude towards society on the part of individuals if they are to achieve goals which they consider socially relevant (see also Parsons 1964: 237–239). The conduct of individuals and groups, which corresponds to these fundamental values, rests on a certain degree of consensus about the institutional order of norms and values. This order is binding on the actor at the same time as it is acknowledged and consciously accepted by him or her.

The educational revolution, in particular, has allowed individuals and societies access to education at all levels, and so enhanced people's ability to act rationally. It has also made it possible for individuals to better employ their knowledge to attain goals and to put values of general interest into practice. The university has become the institutional setting for discussion of the human condition in general terms, and this thanks to the intellectuals who act both within it and outside it. University teaching provides people with the competencies, in the form of specialized knowledge, necessary for practicing a profession and acting within the cultural system. The cultural system is, in fact, an element of the action system. It therefore includes all action components as they are oriented to cultural objects.

Understanding and teaching about cultural objects, as well as the research activities that are focused on them, belong to this system. In the modern society, cultural objects form a stock of meanings. This we term knowledge. It serves as the basis for the cultural system and, within the social system, it relates to the fiduciary subsystem (quadrant L). As previously mentioned, the latter includes four constitutive elements. These can be conceptually placed within the AGIL pattern: the cognitive subsystem A; the "civil religion" system L (a form of secularized religion, some details of which will be provided later); the moral community subsystem I; the *telic* subsystem G, through which the ultimate purposes of the cultural system are symbolically expressed and connected with the other subsystems of the social system.

SOCIOLOGY OF ETHNIC INEQUALITY

Ethnic inequality, in particular, the disadvantaged condition of the African-American minority in the United States, is a theme that Parsons dealt with on several occasions; similarly for the problem of social inequality. In this paragraph, we are concerned with his latest works (Parsons 1969: 252–291; 1977: 381–404). Parsons characterizes an ethnic group according to a dual standard: its specific cultural tradition, and the voluntary nature of membership in that group. An ethnic group shares the following characteristics with other groups: it is a source of identity and a source of widespread and long-lasting solidarity for its members, and it excludes them from belonging to other ethnic groups. These properties, jointly considered, make it a *fiduciary association*. Members are therefore responsible for the protection of this tradition within the broader context of the society to which they belong. This ensures that the group can define and preserve itself as a moral community.

In modern differentiated societies, membership in an ethnic group is voluntary as it results from subjective identification with that group. This identification is often claimed with earnestness, even when this claim is objectively doubtful, i.e., in cases where social class, geographic location, residence in a city or elsewhere, etc. would naturally dissociate an individual from a given ethnic group. Such passionate claims are therefore often merely symbolic. Paradoxically, however, they can result from precisely this questionable identification with an ethnic group. The fact that people claim symbolic ethnic identity is, indeed, evidence of the complexity of modern age social systems, and of the consequent risks of social and normative de-linking, anomy, or loss of identity. The case of the African-American minority in the United States is unique in that it rests on an objective standard, namely, skin color. Still, this, itself, is anything but uniform in those who claim such identity.

African-Americans directly claim identity as an entire ethnic group, i.e., including the quite visible segment of that population who lives in urban ghettoes. Their condition tends to increasingly differentiate them from other African-Americans who are gradually finding their way into the broader American society. For this ethnic group is itself a national community with an ever-growing pluralist social structure, one to which ethnical identity cannot always be so clearly attached. Membership in a group, be it ethnic or religious, does not therefore determine all of the parameters of the social life of an individual. The claim to a Black identity has sometimes taken on a symbolic and militant character in the light of the inclusion and assimilation process that are ongoing for a large part of the African-American minority. However, this claim can be effective only for that increasingly smaller proportion of this ethnic minority that has not yet been assimilated due to economic discrimination and exclusion from political and social rights. And, assimilation does not merely mean inclusion. The former, unlike the latter, is a process that does not undermine cultural identity.

Rather, the process of inclusion assumes that those who benefit from it enjoy full civil and political rights. The Civil Rights Movement of the African-Americans has produced considerable improvements where inclusion is concerned. There is no doubt that they still find themselves disadvantaged in comparison to other ethnic groups, such as the Jewish and the Catholic communities. In the past, the latter were also discriminated against in the United States; they were, however, at least guaranteed equal civil and political rights. The social inclusion process has yet to be completed for the African-American minority in the United States. There are several reasons for this: the past history of slavery and its relative geographical isolation to the southern section of the country; also, there is the problem of the racist and segregationist tendencies which emerged in some American political and religious institutions over time. These have undoubtedly thwarted the process of integration. For the African-American minority, numerous disadvantages have been the result of this: economical, educational, and also in the areas of health, housing and family life. One consequence this is anti-social behaviors. They have, in turn, prevented a part of this minority from being fully included in the national community. Provided it does not encourage separatism, the solidarity that links the members of the African-American community can contribute to the continuation of this assimilation process. History makes it clear that this has been the case with other ethnic groups in the United States.

PARSONS' FURTHER STUDIES IN APPLIED SOCIOLOGY

Parsons carried out still further studies in a variety of areas. We briefly examine them here. They are theoretically oriented, but anchored in the empirical research conducted by other scholars. In the case of the sociology of health, however, Parsons referred to his own studies. Their subjects are varied and heterogeneous. They focus on health, religion, socialization and education, concern the maintenance of the latent pattern of values, and can therefore be classified into the functional quadrant L of the social system. Since it is subject to social control, the problem of human health and access to health services implies possible problems with deviance, control and so also social integration. Quadrant I of the social system therefore becomes relevant. Quadrants I and L of the social system belong to quadrant I on the more general action system. This, in turn, is included in an even larger conceptual framework, namely, that through which Parsons conceptualized the human condition in his last period. Access to health services was also studied by Parsons in previous periods. In particular, in *The Social System* (1951), he maintained that the social positions of patients and doctors are both to be understood in institutional terms.

In subsequent elaborations on this (Parsons 1964a: 236–291; 1978: 17–34, 66–81, 401–405), Parsons once again took up some theses he had previously formulated. However, he also took into account his subsequent contributions to, and refinements of, the AGIL conceptual framework. This is most obviously the case in his late work on the human condition. His definition of health as a social, rather than merely a physical condition, remains substantially unchanged: It is the ability to perform social roles in a satisfactory and effective way. Assessing this ability requires that one take into account the commitment which the patient has made to recover his normal condition. It will have been made bearing in mind the functional needs of the social system in its relations with other action systems (cultural, personality, and organism) and with external systems (e.g., physical-chemical). Social control mechanisms intervene when this assessment is negative and they do so in keeping with the standards established by the cultural system (Parsons 1964a: 125, 265–282; 1978: 69).

Among the theoretical propositions he restated, the following are noteworthy: a) The doctor's and the patient's social positions are characterized by the recognition of the positive value of health, the negative value of illness, and the active commitment on the part of both of them to achieve a condition of good health for the patient, b) The doctor carries out a professional activity which adheres to universalistic norms of conduct. It is oriented to collective values, rather than to the professional's interest. It has a functionally specific character. In fact, a doctor's relation with a patient is exclusively aimed at attaining the patient's health. For this, the doctor and the patient are jointly responsible. The doctor exerts social control over the patient only in this respect, c) The patients' role implies that he or she is obligated to demonstrate their trust in the doctor; to cooperate to attain his or her own recovery; and then to immediately take up again the roles they could not perform during the period of illness.

The conceptual and theoretical elements which Parsons introduces in his last works are remarkable: a) The doctor, like any other professional, has a *fiduciary responsibility* toward the client, in this case, the patient. This responsibility is shared with the patient, who must cooperate with the doctor, but also with the healthcare institution in which the doctor is working, b) Illness is evidenced in the incapacity of a living system to perform appropriately in relation to a plurality of human and non-human environments, some of which are beyond its control. Therefore, in the context of his general analysis of the human condition, Parsons conceives of health as a symbolic, socially acquired and employed, circulation medium among the organisms (physical-chemical and organic), the human actor's personality, and the other elements of the social system.

With reference to the American "nuclear" family of the 1950s and 1960s, family is considered an institution which performs the essential function of socialization, by deflecting children's eroticism toward a parent of the opposite sexual gender and by guiding them to take up adult roles in varying institutional environments. Parental role differentiation drives the mother to take care of her children, while the father, the head of a family, is assigned an occupational role outside the family. This differentiation involves the transformation of the family from a unit of production into a unit of consumption. As a further consequence, and also due to geographic mobility, families have become more isolated in comparison to previous generations. Despite frequent predictions to the contrary, there are no signs of dissolution of the family unit. However, the current high divorce rate definitely point to the fact that it is strained. (Parsons 1964a: 212–217; see also Parsons 1955 and Lidz 2000: 407–408).

Parsons defined socialization as a process through which individuals develop both their motivation to conform to social values and their commitment and abilities to perform social roles (Parsons 1964: 130). This theme had interested him from the time he wrote *The Social System*. We here briefly mention some of the essays which he wrote in the following years. They deal with school and peer groups, respectively considered to be formal and informal socialization agencies (Parsons 1964a: 129–182; see Alexander 1987: 82–88). School, especially the primary school, socializes the youth to the value of achievement, which is evaluated against objective standards. It also prepares young people to make adult decisions and take responsibilities, and thus moves him to ward autonomy from his family of origin. The family has been subject to heavy strains as a result of social change. As noted, the high divorce rate is an indication of this. These strains have negatively affected its functioning. Peer groups lead youths toward autonomy and away from adults' control; they also provide him with new sources of approval and social acceptance.

Both of these are institutions of socialization which offset possible strain on the young originating from less than satisfactory educational achievements, greater expectations placed upon them in the educational field and the new found autonomy from the family. In fact, the school holds to universal, and therefore impartial, standards of evaluation, whereas the peer group makes use of standards of evaluation and prestige which are different from the school's. They combine independence from parental expectations, which can reveal itself through deviant behaviors with pressures to conform. These positive functions are offset to some extent by the strains caused in the young both by their differing levels of access to higher education and by their insecurity. The latter stems from the fast pace of social changes and their lack of power and influence.

Religion, especially when it is institutionalized, is also a source of social integration; it also inculcates values and norms, even in our secular age. In the Western world, this process evidences itself as privatization (or individualization) of the sacred in the form of *civil religion*. Where this occurs, there are no references to symbols and beliefs belonging to particular creeds and religious traditions. Instead, actors show a widely shared attachment and commitment to the social system as a whole in so far as they consider it a moral community. The solidarity that results is systemic and it has moral implications which rest on rationally defensible beliefs. This unique civil religion is compatible both with institutionalized individualism and with a pluralistic social structure and ethic. And, all of these are the hallmarks of a secular society, one which is penetrated by a rationally defensible ethic compatible with technological rationality. If they conform to these cognitive and normative conditions, the new religious movements that introduce integration into a secularized society can assert themselves and become institutionalized. (Parsons 1970: 519–21; 1978: 232–63, 300–22).

THE AMERICAN UNIVERSITY SYSTEM

Finally, it is worth mentioning the study Parsons carried out in cooperation with Gerald M. Platt. It focuses on the American university system. This is not only the last work published by Parsons, but also a study that thoroughly employs the theoretical apparatus developed during the last two periods of his production. As mentioned in the Technical Appendix at the end of this work

(Parsons 1978: 435–440), the circulation and interchange media that can be identified at the level of general action theory (summarized in a cybernetic information and control hierarchy by the acronym LIGA) do not coincide with those that can be identified at the analytically less abstract level of the social subsystem. In fact, the latter is included in the general theory of action and forms the internal environment of the action system. Parsons formulates the following propositions with respect to the interchange system at the level of general action theory:

The cultural system L provides the organism A with standards of cognitive validity and significance; in exchange it receives judgments of relevance. Interchange between the organism A and the personality system G, in which the cognitive function holds supremacy, involves control exerted by the organism A over cognitive capacity and competence. At the same time, the personality A provides the opportunity to learn to act effectively and to apply its competencies in an intelligent way toward the achievement of different objectives. The cultural subsystem L provides the social subsystem I with the institutionalization of solidarity insofar as it takes into account the moral standards established by the cultural subsystem and regulates the voluntary commitment to solidarity. The latter is strengthened by sentiments of justice. Moreover, the cultural subsystem L provides the personality system G with the adopted expressive standards and the meanings relating to personal style; in exchange, it receives the identity and modes of revelation that character- ize this style. Lastly, Parsons jointly considers the interchanges between the organism A and the social subsystem I. These are the relations between the cognitive and the affective complex. They take place while these two com- plexes are engaged in cognitive activities within the societal community.

THE SOCIOLOGY OF UNIVERSITY EDUCATION

Parsons' studies on the university system in the United States and elsewhere (France, Great Britain) occupied him throughout the last decade of his life. As he stated, this investigation was suggested to him in part by accidental circum- stances when he served as President of the American Academy of Arts and Sciences from 1967 onward. In this position, Parsons established intellectual exchanges with several representatives of a variety of branches of learning and interests. From this he drew an increased commitment to interdisciplinary research and a great openness in his cognitive orientation. This would not have been possible otherwise. He recalls the decision taken by the journal Daedalus, the official organ of the American Academy of Arts and Sciences, to carry out a study on the current condition of higher education in modern society. But, these biographical and accidental events aside, Parsons had basically a strong scientific interest in the university, both as an agent of socialization to the values of knowledge and its progress, and as an institutional setting for the practice of the academic profession (Parsons 1970: 509–513). This interest is born out in a theoretical monograph co-authored with Gerald M. Platt, *The American University* (Parsons, Platt 1973) and in some other, more empirically-oriented writings published between 1973 and 1977. The latter were eventually collected under the title *Sociology of Higher Education* in the second part of *Action Theory and the Human Condition* (Parsons 1978: 91–164).

Higher education and research, which are primary and specific functions of the university, grant it a double institutionalized status as a guardian of the cultural tradition of modern society and a place in which the *cognitive complex* is formed and preserved. As mentioned in the Technical Appendix (Parsons 1978: 423–447), this complex is analyzed as belonging, within the AGIL general action system, to the cultural system L as a foundation of cognitive validity and significance, and to the fiduciary subsystem of the social system I. The cognitive complex is unitary despite the current trend toward specialization within the disciplines. The cultural system consists of a complex of meanings which are stabilized and communicated by a linguistic code regardless of the particular non-cognitive contexts in which action takes place. The cognitive complex is characterized by a kind of cognitive rationality. This rationality requires the existence of a differentiated system of institutionalized values shared by the cultural and the social systems. In this way, these two systems can become linked and interpenetrate and strengthen each other.

Cognitive rationality can express itself by encouraging individual achievement and redefining values where necessary. The latter are institutionalized in the higher education system, the American university system in particular. They are consistent with those of economic rationality. Therefore, in the United States the same system of values has promoted research and teaching along with the goal of academic production However, the university can become a moral community and this in two ways. First, if it succeeds in preserving its commitment to the values of cognitive rationality. This can happen either directly, with the pursuit of pure knowledge (quadrant L of the general action system), or indirectly, through those who make use of cognitive rationality as an absolutely necessary source of knowledge and experience. The applied professions are a case in point: medicine (quadrant G, because of its interest in individuals' health), engineering (quadrant A, because of its interest in adaptation to the physical environment), and law (quadrant I, considering its interest in the normative structure of social order). Secondly, it if it succeeds in preserving commitment to the value of loyalty toward the institution. Furthermore, it is necessary to preserve the university's independence from society as a whole, the latter being considered a moral community in a different and more extensive sense than the university.

The cognitive complex relates the cultural system to the social system. It appeals to the values of knowledge and competence and to that of rationality when it comes to evaluating the truth of a proposition. These values are institutionalized in the university (quadrant L of the general action system). This complex makes use of generalized symbolic interchange media. They have their own code and symbolic structure and operate in a specific cognitive context; at the same time they circulate throughout the entire general action system. These generalized symbolic interchange media consist in: intelligence, performance capacity, and definition of the situation. The latter implies selection according to cultural, moral, cognitive standards of relevance. It precludes any commitment to alternative situations; moreover, as a medium of generalized symbolic interchange it circulates throughout the whole action system. This definition pertains to intellectuals, who, in contrast to the representatives of professions, are not specialized in a particular branch of knowledge, but are responsible for ensuring the normative validity of the social order (quadrant L of the general action system). They also evaluate it according to certain standards of moral and cognitive rationality (quadrant I of the general action system), set social goals and identify the ways of attaining them (quadrant G of the general action system).

Intelligence is not meant to be understood here as an attribute of the individual. It is rather a symbolic regulator of the processes through which the necessary cognitions and competencies for producing and implementing knowledge are formed in the individual personality; and thereby objectives are attained. Performance capacity is the ability to rationally act in a competent and appropriate way in a situation and, in general, when confronted with a significant normative order. This capacity is relevant not only in cognitive contexts, but also in affective and moral ones. The academic community is institutionally rooted in the fiduciary system, because it is assigned the function of preserving, developing and putting into practice the knowledge and other elements that jointly form the cognitive complex. For the other sectors of the social system with which it has an interchange, it produces resources that, when combined with others, facilitate the performance of socially relevant functions. An example if this is the creation of a skilled workforce that is committed to carrying out its professional functions. At the level of the general action system, which includes the social system, the academic community produces knowledge and competence. It also intelligently organizes affective interests, intelligence being intended here in the aforementioned sense.

In the United States, the university, particularly the Graduate Schools of Arts and Sciences, is an institutional setting in which the cognitive complex, and hence also the value of cognitive rationality, is shaped and preserved. The university is part of a complex society. Its prestige and influence have grown along with the increasingly greater import assigned to the cognitive complex, and consequently also to knowledge, individual competence, and intelligence. In America, institutionalization of the cognitive complex in which knowledge is pursued for its own sake, has led to a focus on teaching and research. It has also placed students in the impersonal and transitory position of "those who must learn," and this within the organizational sphere of the academic department. All this differs, however, from the European practice of establishing a personal and long-lasting relation between a professor and a student in the context of specialized university institutes.

The evolution of educational institutions has taken place, as has social evolution in general, in terms of adaptive upgrading, inclusion, and value generalization. This process has been accompanied by the evolution of students' personality. Students who attend college are still undergraduates and so at the beginning of their university studies. Over time, however, they can gradually upgrade their cognitive capacity and competence in various intellectual disciplines as their studies require; similarly for their concomitant ability to deal with an increasingly differentiated external environment. The differentiation and independence of their personalities corresponds to a similar level of differentiation in the social environment and in their curriculum. The socialization process is thus accomplished both within the family and the college. It makes it possible for young people to exert more intelligent, rational control over their actions; to relate to their professors (and so to avoid mutual antagonism); and to identify themselves with the institution of the university and eventually take on greater responsibilities in matters of common interest, such as university management.

For college students, therefore, the value of institutionalized individualism, as shared by the larger societal community, can and does assert itself. Moreover, the freedom to act in this community, as it is represented by the university institution, allows them to achieve the highest level of differentiation and social integration. This occurs through the performance of complementary functions in a differentiated environment. Individual personalities, in their cognitive, affective and evaluative aspects, are centered on the value of cognitive rationality. It asserts itself in evaluating alternative courses of action. However, neither individual personalities, nor the academic community as a whole with its own institutionalized values of cognitive rationality and academic freedom, are allowed to prevail.

The academic community is that part of society which is responsible for enforcing the value of cognitive rationality and answering to it before the societal community. General educational programs are not directly connected to problems or to their solutions, but are essential for developing students' competence and intelligence. These programs are the cognitive nucleus of the academic system. From point of view of the university as an institution, it is advisable that this cognitive nucleus be accompanied by non-cognitive engagements and interests on the part of the students. These interests should be external to this cognitive nucleus, and in general, to the students' curriculum. They may have distinct personal, political and social content. By cultivating them, it is possible to strengthen one's intellectual abilities and better take part in civil and political society. The secondary school shares these same values with the college: objective standards of evaluation, a moral commitment to cognitive rationality and guidance on action, and the recognition of moral authority. The latter can always be challenged in the name of cognitive rationality.

The values that are institutionalized in the secondary school are consistent with those of the higher educational system. In the latter, there is greater autonomy, social differentiation, and a pluralism of generalized values, but less emphasis on hierarchical social structure and normative integration among students, faculty and administration. Hence, in the context of higher education, socialization takes place under conditions of strain. Students often react to it by opposing their teachers with a strict moral and cognitive absolutism, an absolutism that denies them any kind of justice and truth, and reveals a widespread egalitarian solidarity that excludes any other person, loyalty and affection. The result is a re-compacting, or de-differentiation, process across the cultural and in the social systems. This tends to delegitimize the higher education system overall. Its cognitive nucleus is, as noted, based on universal values and thereby influences the development of specialized knowledge and its competent application.

In the United States, professional schools are a constitutive part of the university system, e.g., the schools of engineering, medicine and law. In such institutions, the most long-standing and established professions are taught, but also some more recent ones, such as public and private administration, social work, and corporate management. The relevance of the cognitive complex to the American university system has led to a cultural orientation that gives great importance and stresses professionals' competence and integrity values. This is also the case for the applied professions. However, in the United States as in Europe, research in purely academic areas has gradually differentiated itself from research and teaching of its applications. Similarly, the discipline of medicine has abandoned its original and exclusive concern with illnesses as a biological problem, and has expanded to include the study of psychological or psychiatric subjects, such as psychoanalysis. It has done this by increasing the required level of basic scientific training/education, and consequently, by redirecting its investments in equipment, laboratories and staff.

The legal profession, training for which is traditionally provided at universities both in Europe and in the United States, distinguishes itself from others by the fact that its decisions are made binding on the public through the political system by means of the police, courts and the prison system. In Anglo-Saxon countries, judges and lawyers enjoy a public status. As in the case of the medical profession, a professional lawyer exerts moral authority over his client and makes use of a set of procedures and specialized knowledge to define the client's legal situation. Furthermore, the relation between the professional (such as a doctor or a lawyer) and the client is marked by a technical-cognitive and emotional component. It is protected by confidentiality; whereas communication flows freely among professionals. The general recognition of their cognitive foundations distinguishes both professions from others of more recent origin, such as the educator, the social worker, and the corporate or public administrator. Engineers, distinguish themselves from other professionals, e.g. doctors, because they have a unique social responsibility toward the physical environment,

Medicine, engineering and law are applied professions which put their knowledge at the service of their clients. But, each profession focuses on problems concerning the meaning of knowledge and competence as these relate to the human condition. Professions like the academic one are anchored in the most general level of the action systems, since they are in charge of protecting the central cognitive resources of a society. Others, e.g. teaching, social work, business administration, and various lines of work related to corporate management, perform non–cognitive functions within the social system. Instances thereof are adaptation to the physical environment (engineering); the health of the individual (medicine); and normative order integrity and social adaptation (law). As noted, training for these is made available through the university. Students of these disciplines are encouraged to achieve advanced knowledge and high levels of competency, thus conforming to the prevailing university standards and honoring the value of cognitive rationality. Intelligence, as a generalized circulation medium for the solution of cognitive problems, and affection, as a medium for maintaining solidarity in the social system, must be set into mutual functional equilibrium.

In addition to intelligence, performance capacity, and affection, the fourth generalized symbolic interchange medium among the elements of the general actions system (the organism, personality, social and cultural systems) is the definition of a situation. It is devoid of any specific content and, once provided, it excludes all alternative definitions. It is developed by intellectuals, who in most cases are not only academicians, and therefore persons lacking in the specialized technical skills of applied science, but whose task it is to ensure the meaning for, and provide an evaluation of, the cultural symbolic systems. Generally, they address all of the problems of the human condition. Intellectuals thus perform both a moral and an expressive function. They rely upon the definition of a situation in interchanges in a plurality of contexts: cognitive (an action is intelligent if it complies with standards of cognitive validity and significance), moral (an action is moral if it complies with institutionalized moral standards and with the collectively recognized sense of justice), and cultural (an action is significant if it complies with situational requirements, cultural standards and individual motivations).

Definitions of the situation are provided at the level of the general action system. This level is marked by a conflict between the process of rationalization, on the one hand, and the formation of the personality and individuality, on the other. The university system, in which the social and the cultural systems intertwine, acts as a "bank" or a reserve of the intelligence that circulates in the action systems. This reserve grows through the transfer of deposits (e.g., students or professors entrust their cognitive interests to the university institution). The stability of the system may be then negatively affected by a process of intelligence inflation. Conferring loyalty and commitment on the academic system in order to put its values into effect would necessarily involve increased costs. This reserve of intelligence can however also decrease because of withdrawals or disinvestments from the cognitive complex. Anti-intellectual attitudes among the student population, together with mistrust of the legitimacy of independently pursued intellectual interests often trigger this; similarly for mistrust of the cognitive capacities of members of the university community and doubt about the value of knowledge in general.

Such a "deflation" process, i.e., a diminished appreciation of intelligence, and consequently of the academic system itself, has taken place among college students, and, paradoxically, in a period of quantitative expansion of the institutions of higher education. These institutions, whose function it is to provide a favorable environment for the discovery and learning, require an academic staff committed to these values as well if they are to perform this function. An institution's successful performance involves, in turn, academic freedom and role stability. The inflation and deflation processes can affect all hierarchy levels of the cybernetic control. At the highest level (cultural), excessive expectations for the ability of cognitive culture to solve general problems have produced a new awareness of the different dangers posed by, and the inconveniences caused by scientific and technologic progress. At the level of the general action system (culture, personality and organism), both the growing number of students enrolled in higher education and prestige which increasingly attaches to it, have produced two notable results: cognitive inflation and lesser commitment to study on the part of students, and their decreased involvement in the university institution. These developments have also frustrated expectations of rewards for those who have achieved a high level of educational qualification. And, such frustrations are the source of the student unrest (Parsons' essay was written in the 1970s).

At the level of the social system, and of the societal community in general, there has, from the point of view of teaching staff, been depreciation both in intelligence and in influence, the major generalized circulation and exchange media of the university. The teaching staff has proved to be increasingly less prepared to deal with widespread reluctance on the part of students, especially those less advanced in their studies, to commit themselves to traditional educational programs. Conservative representatives of the political system have reacted negatively both to student activism (e.g. their impossible requests), and to their unrest (occupation of the universities). One result of this has been a reduction in the public funds allocated to universities, and this in a period of growing costs. Intellectuals, students and politicians have questioned the values, organization and purposes of university education. The institutionalized value of cognitive rationality in the university system is often considered irrelevant or even dangerous; the hierarchical and authoritative structure of the educational system is judged excessive or inadequate; the purposes of providing education have been criticized as serving primarily the ruling class, and discriminating against the weaker segments of society. Finally, the content of this educational experience, insofar as it is not connected with matters of general interest, is sometimes taken to be irrelevant.

The American university system has certain unique characteristics. Both college and advanced students are taught by the same faculty; general education courses taught in the Graduate Schools of Arts and Sciences are integrated with those taught in the professional schools; and, finally, there is a homogeneity of values, and no central state authority is in place to oversee the educational process, as is the case in Continental Europe. Since the nineteenth century, American institutions of higher education have gradually evolved into this bundle of distinctive learning opportunities. Current criticism aims to simplify it, or to remove some of its seeming superfluous elements. However, the institutions of the university system, taken together with the notion of academic freedom and the stability of teaching positions, constitute a social system. And, it is one which encourages intellectual work and other general academic functions. Furthermore, the university system is not compatible with certain types of institutional change. It ought not, for example, be subject to market conditions or bureaucratic modes of management; its cognitive function ought to remain its central concern; it should also not be subordinated to the political, expressive or moral goals of society as a whole. Lastly, it should not maintain a rigid separation between teaching and research.

Changes of this sort, if they were to occur, would lead to a devaluation, or "deflation," of the university system, possibly to such a point that it could no longer satisfactorily perform its educational and cognitive functions. Instead, changes should be introduced with a view to improving its functional capacity by adaptive upgrading and increased commitment, at a social system level, so as to ensure better performance of its cognitive functions. This could be achieved through the opening up of new fields of research, by combining academic and non-academic interests, through openness to interdisciplinary studies, increasing differentiation of the curriculum and generalization of values. The result does not have necessarily to be a repudiation of cognitive rationality as a value. On the contrary, cognitive interests must retain their traditional primacy in the institution of the university along with their associated functions, if the academic system is to be preserved.

In terms of Parsons' conceptual system, a condition of moderate cognitive inflation (as was the case after World War II until the 1960s), has been marked by a relative equilibrium in the interchanges among the cultural L, the social I, the personality G and the organism A subsystems. The educational revolution has produced considerable and long-lasting investments in intelligence (i.e. the ability to apply one's knowledge through acquired skills), and so caused many people to restrict their goals and postpone their rewards in order to maximize their cognitive competences. An inflation of intelligence (1968–1970) was followed by a deflationary period. It was accompanied by the request to re-address investments in intelligence which were aimed at non-cognitive symbols. This, in turn, has affected the social system I and the personality system G.

The conclusion of this work was written by Parsons' colleague and collaborator Neil J. Smelser. He summarizes some of the theses formulated by Parsons in this book and in other works:

1. Concerning *Toward a General Theory of Action*, *The American University* and *The Social System*, Smelser remarks that the social system is the result of the intertwining of a plurality of subsystems, each with its own specific functional requirements. In so far as it stresses the institutionalized value of cognitive rationality, the academic subsystem has contributed to the development of an educational revolution. Together with the industrial and democratic revolution, this has been one of the most important processes of structural change in modern societies. However, it is also hardly compatible with these other values, as it measures the value of achievement in cognitive terms.

   The result has been the pursuit of high academic quality and prestige on the part of the teaching staff; but also conflict between the teaching staff itself and the university organizations which favor open admissions, and also harsh competition within the educational institutions themselves. On the other hand, the values of cognitive rationality and professional achievement, when measured against universal standards, remain essential to the collective principle of the university as an association of peers. This is what distinguishes the academic profession and lends it respect; it is also what defines the organization of modern universities. Smelser considers it advisable to integrate Parsons' aforementioned theses, and he remarks that, in educational institutions, the collective principle co-exists with bureaucratic control; which is gaining ground in the university. Educational staff is therefore put on the defensive vis-à-vis administrative authorities.

2. With reference to the changes that occurred in the American higher education system in the 1970s, Smelser aims at integrating the thesis advanced by both Parsons and Platt. According to them, the academic principle of preserving commitment to cognitive rationality is what keeps the system united. It makes it impossible to define the academic institution merely as a market in which goods and services are exchanged. Hence, it ensures that the structural differentiation is retained between research (which is relevant for advanced graduate students) and teaching (which is instead relevant for undergraduate students). As Smelser notes, should this distinction be blurred, it would deprive the university of the economic support provided by its former students, and consequently, of essential funds for research. But, the quantitative and functional expansion of the university has taken place without such structural differentiation. It has limited first and foremost general education, in order to benefit professional schools and research programs. This has led, in the first place, the decline of the general education function, entrusted to the secondary school, for the benefit of professional and research schools. Secondly, teaching and educational functions may though they formally remaining the responsibility of the teaching staff; however, they come to be performed by non-institutional staff because of the excessive workloads of institutional faculty.

3. Concerning the socialization process carried out within the college, Smelser does not think that colleges and universities constitute a *moral community* in the Parsonian sense. Many of these institutions are, in fact, isolated from the surrounding community. In addition, relations among students, on the one hand, and among professors and administrators on the other, are too transitory to allow students to identify with their educational institutions. Rather than explaining students' unrest as a rebellion against intellectual work and academic functions in general, Smelser prefers to underline the contrast between the expectations that higher education had produced in students, and students' inadequate socialization. The latter resulted from the fragmentation of university authority, and also from

the fact that resources at the disposal of lower level universities are often insufficient. Hence, these expectations, based initially on affective overinvestment, have remained unfulfilled.

THE REMAINING ESSAYS ON
THE SOCIOLOGY OF EDUCATION

As mentioned, in the 1970s Parsons wrote numerous essays on the topic of the sociology of education. They have a more markedly empirical orientation than does the work discussed above. For purposes of reference, however, the latter is considered his major work (Parsons, Platt 1973). These later essays, all of which are preceded by a concise introduction, concern the future of the university and the growth of the American higher education and research system. They also discuss its distinctive characteristics and aspects of its stability and capacity for change (Parsons 1978: 91–164). We wish to briefly mention them here and delineate both the elements of their continuity and those characteristics which distinguish them from his major work.

The first essay reconstructs the history of the changes that took place in the American education system with reference to higher education and research after the Civil War, in particular, its expansion in the early 1970s. Parsons then considers the organizational innovation which occurred in the United States to the Department (compared to European universities), and the organizational and hierarchical differentiation between: a) Undergraduates and graduates, b) Elite universities and others, c) Research and teaching, and d) The mutually incompatible principles of the collective association of peers and the hierarchical structure of bureaucratic organization. He here argues a thesis that is dealt with more extensively in the essay on the American university, namely that of the primacy of the institutions. In his opinion, this was subject to question at the time. However, as can still be observed, the values of cognitive rationality, teaching and research freedom, and collective association have prevailed.

Parsons' essay on the growth of the American system of higher education and research considers its the development in the United States. He focuses in particular on the most prestigious universities. He also outlines its history and hints at a brief explanation of this growth by comparing it with corresponding European systems. As he notes, this development was begun in the 1890s, continued until the 1930s, and began again after World War II. The American higher education system has been characterized by a commitment to purely academic teaching, i.e., it has not included any practical training/educational purposes within the departments of Arts and Sciences. It is in them that the most varied kinds of teaching have been done, ranging from classical arts to the natural and social sciences, and professional studies. And, the quality is often very high. This has encouraged a growing number of students to attend these courses, as they preferred not to limit their education to the high-school diploma. They thereby obtain an advantage in the labor market as well.

How can this quantitative and qualitative development be explained? The multi-factorial explanation proposed by Parsons is not only worked out from an economic point of view (i.e., by exclusively considering benefits expected from private companies, who, in turn, expect to make a profit from their investments in education), but involves two additional non-economic factors: First, the Protestant moral tradition has brought with it a predisposition for rational and intellectual culture. Secondly, the drive toward economic and cultural development has always been a pronounced hallmark of the American culture and has found expression in the economic-philosophic tradition of Utilitarianism, in the ideology of entrepreneurial freedom, and in the rational pursuit of economic benefits. This tradition, with its unique ideology and practice, has led to a decentralized system of higher education and research. It stands in contrast to the European systems but accords with the processes of differentiation and institutionalization that correspond to two forms of rationality: economic and cognitive.

Another consequence of this course of development has been that universities are chosen (e.g. instead of scientific academies) to be the institutional setting in which higher education is made available. This kind of education, generally prestigious, has attracted American citizens eager to obtain an educational qualification which makes it possible for them to compete with the education provided by the most renowned and culturally respected European universities. Many wealthy and learned Americans identify with these academic standards. Parsons mentions some outstanding examples of this, e.g., T.S. Eliot, the James brothers and Henry Adams. Between the best European and American universities there has always been intellectual exchange and mutual emulation, all of it to their mutual advantage. In particular, American universities have embraced the European model of an institution which is the locus of non-specialized, non-technical knowledge. Thus even though they had been originally conceived as specialized institutions for technical education (e.g., the Massachusetts Institute of Technology), they have gradually begun to be open to including other disciplines, especially the social sciences such as economics.

In another essay, Parsons dwells upon the "bundle" of disciplines taught in the American universities. These disciplines distinguish themselves by the variety of the courses offered. They are organized by departments which are partially independent of one another, and defined by the fact that research is institutionalized and also by the fact that they serve the specific function of providing pure (non-applied) science, competence and cognitive standards to different categories of persons, especially intellectuals. Finally, this bundle of disciplines distinguishes itself by its tendency to establish national and international associations among specialists from the same disciplines or those which are interdisciplinary nature.

The knowledge that universities disseminate is subject to control through cognitive canons (or standards) of validity and significance. It is connected by intelligence as a generalized symbolic medium of interchange that can be converted into influence and knowledge. These canons are binding for scholars and researchers, and in general for all those who are professionally and permanently committed to the pursuit of rational knowledge. The organizational pre-eminence of the body of knowledge taught in the American universities, together with the absence of clearly defined disciplinary orientations, have developed in conjunction with the rapidly expanding emphasis on theoretical knowledge. If it is to preserve and combine different personal competencies and thus build a societal community, this system must be differentiated according to occupational roles and disciplinary competences. Their cultivation requires considerable investment of time, and a commitment to a complex educational process, one which is harmonious and free of internal friction.

Finally, the essay concerning stability and change in the American university aims at evaluating the consequences of the period of student unrest of the years 1972–1974. Parsons asks whether and how much the organizational and institutional nucleus of the elite universities has been changed by this, and concludes that it has not been substantially undermined. The arguments he puts forward are the following: First, the bundle of disciplines taught in these universities has not been shattered, and so the continuity and strength of university teaching has been preserved. Secondly, the principles of neutrality and the pre-eminent value of disinterested knowledge have also been preserved along with the intellectual commitment thereto shown by advanced students. And, this has happened, despite severe criticism from extremist students. The research function has also maintained its pre-eminence among academicians, who still garner prestige from the scientific results of their work.

The trend toward egalitarianism, which began in the 1960s in conjunction with the Civil Rights Movement, has led to an increase in the share of women and representatives of ethnic minorities on the teaching staffs of American universities. Other innovations have, however, proved less successful. In fact, no formal equality has prevailed between teachers and students where decisions on administration and teaching are concerned. Teachers' attempts to unionize have also proved unsuccessful because their scientific achievements have remained the primary standard for promotion. The current decrease in student unrest may be transitory, but the changes to American university system still represent an important contributing factor in the development of American social structure and culture. And radical changes are not likely to be forthcoming. The interpretation put forward by Parsons and Platt in their work *The American University,* according to which a period of moderate inflation would be followed by an opposite period of deflation, can, from the point of view of a devaluation of cognitive purposes, explain at least in part, the present period of relative calm.

These essays on the higher education system in the United States summarize and integrate some themes and theses from Parsons' major works (Parsons, Platt 1973). The following elements of conceptual continuity are of note: a) the notion of the university as an institutional setting in which rational and pure knowledge is pursued in a variety of disciplines, b) the category of intelligence, as a symbolic medium of circulation and interchange, c) the concepts of inflation and deflation, in the peculiar sense that Parsons assigns to these terms. From a thematic point of view, the elements of continuity between these essays and the major works are: a) the quantitative growth of colleges and universities in America after World War II, b) their ever-increasing functional and organizational differentiation, c) the students riots of the 1960s and 1970s, d) the possible negative consequences of student unrest for the performance of college and university functions.

In summary, in the essays discussed here there are some new elements which integrate and complete Parsons' thought in *The American University.* In fact, greater attention is paid to a comparison with the European universities and to the reasons for the particular attraction that they held for some young Americans until the 1920s. The causes of quantitative growth of colleges and universities in the United States, and of the period of relative calm after the student riots, are also explained in detail. Here, in contrast to in *The American University,* Parsons seems to pay less attention to intellectuals, to the formation of a societal community and the development of conceptual patterns.

CONCLUDING REMARKS

This chapter has provided a review of Parsons' writings in the area of applied sociology. These essays cannot be considered to be the fruit of empirical research, in the sense commonly given to this term, but rather of an application of the AGIL conceptual pattern to problems of political sociology, social and ethnic inequality, family, education, and religion. As regards Germany on the eve of and after the rise of Nazism, he stresses the anomic condition of the country, a consequence of the incompatibility of Germany's modern class structure and her cultural system, the latter being oriented to its pre-industrial past. The economic instability and the political divisions the existed in that country after the military defeat were also factors. Similarly, the temporary post-World War II success of the right-wing political movement in the U.S., as it was promoted by Senator Joseph McCarthy, can be explained as the outcome of decreased confidence in democracy on the part of the lower middle class.

As Parsons observes, had this movement been successful, it would have led to a "deflation" or a devaluation of political power. This would have had troublesome consequences for the differentiated American political system. Parsons does not mistrust the American democratic institutions, however. In a review of C. Wright Mills,' *The Power Elite*, he writes that the author is mistaken in maintaining that the United States is governed by a small number of corporations, politicians, and military elite, and that the government and the parliament are deprived of power. Power, Parsons argues, is a resource for pursuing collective interest, so an increase in the power of some persons does not involve an equivalent loss for others. A differentiated society, such as the American one, demands an equally differentiated political system, generalized trust, and a system of values capable of supporting it. Inequality can be justified if the social system forms a moral community. This implies that equal opportunities are institutionally guaranteed and legitimized by a widely shared system of values. Integrity and competence are particularly relevant and are supported by a widespread commitment to their implementation.

Professional practice involves an institutionalized adherence to these values and a commitment to putting them into practice in relations with the public as it avails itself of their services. The changes that resulted from the rise of modernity through the three revolutions (industrial, democratic, and educational) are compatible with these values of integrity and competence. They are also compatible with the American values of *institutionalized individualism* and *instrumental activism*, as these are taught by the institutions of socialization. Putting them into effect assumes the complete inclusion of everyone in a citizenship system, a goal which has only been partially fulfilled in the case of some ethnic groups such as Afro-Americans. The value of cognitive rationality is also compatible with American values, particularly as it is taught by the universities. Parsons' interest in these institutions, and in the cognitive complex that they can create and maintain, is evidenced in several of his writings published during the 1970s. The generalized symbolic media of interchange that can be found in the cognitive complex, especially intelligence and influence, circulate throughout the entire action system. According to Parsons, some of the changes to the American university system recently proposed by different sources could undermine its educational and cognitive functions.

Chapter Six

The Reception of Parsons' Work

THE RECEPTION OF PARSONS' WORK: GENERAL REMARKS

Parsons has attracted far more critical attention than most other contemporary sociologists. The secondary literature concerning his work is very extensive, but several introductions to it are noteworthy (see Alexander 1983a: 128–135; 1987: 280–285; Bortolini 1998; Holton 1986b; 2001: 159–161; Holmwood 2006a; Lidz 2000: 423–428; Rocher 1974: 152–167; Sciulli, Gerstein 1985; Turner 1986b). In this chapter, we only consider the reception of certain of his works addressing particular themes. We also summarize critical remarks and discuss interpretations of his work in general terms. Since we here present but do not evaluate the reception of his work reference will be made to extant favorable or critical evaluations. Furthermore, we do not here take upon ourselves the almost impossible task of providing a complete survey of this secondary literature. The works we have selected therefore include only those interpretative and exegetic contributions that we consider particularly relevant to a discussion of his thought.

Some, in particular, have attracted, specific attention, and we wish to briefly mention the secondary literature that explicitly addresses them. We refer in particular to: 1) "Prolegomena to a Theory of Social Institutions," published in 1990, but written in 1934; 2) *The Structure of Social Action*, first published in 1937; 3) *The Social System*, published in 1951; 4) Parsons' economic sociology, with reference not only to the so-called *Marshall Lectures*, but also to *Economy and Society* and related exegetical literature; 5) Parsons' production of the 1960s, in which the evolutionary theory of social change was formulated; 6) His theoretical and applied sociological work of the 1970s, namely, *The Human Condition, The American University*, and

American Society. However, we do not strictly follow this order in presenting the secondary literature when it deals with different works conjointly.

THE FIRST TWO PERIODS OF HIS PRODUCTION (1928–1963)

A non-negligible part of this secondary literature has discussed the relation of continuity or discontinuity between these two periods, although some commentators have considered this kind of discussion scholastic and unfruitful for the progress of sociological theory (Turner 1986: 186). A great deal of attention has been paid, in particular, to Parsons' biographical experience and his works from the years which preceded, accompanied and followed the publication of *The Structure of Social Action* (1937), and also up to and including *The Social System* (1951). In what follows, we present a concise summary of this remarkable secondary literature.

CAMIC'S THESIS

Among the works that preceded *The Structure of Social Action*, the article "Prolegomena to a Theory of Social Institutions" (1934) counters, as mentioned, a subjective method of studying institutions with an objective one. This contribution was worked out and presented by Charles Camic, who set it within a biographical and historical context (Camic 1990a; see also 1991: xxx-xliv; 1992: 427–435). According to Camic (1991), in selecting his sources for this article, Parsons would have made use of a standard adhered to by Harvard economists. In 1934, Parsons was a young instructor of modest academic standing, and an expert in a discipline (sociology) that Harvard had not yet scientifically endorsed. Institutional economists focused on the study of economic institutions such as enterprises, contracts or property rights. After it was proposed by Veblen, a "non-orthodox" economist (not someone who represented marginalist economic theory at the time), this field of study later began to attract the keen interest of anthropologists, economists, psychologists and other students of social science. Parsons himself had been exposed to this kind of teaching when he was attending the college (Camic 1991: xiv-vii).

However, in subsequent years, Parsons would have rejected this teaching as a result of his contacts with Harvard economists. In keeping with their view of economics, he judged the institutionally recognized study of economics to be poorly grounded epistemologically, and therefore lacking in scientific credibility. By contrast to this formerly prevailing approach a sociological one grounds the study of institutions in shared and fundamental values. Camic makes this observation in reference to Parsons. This requires turning one's attention to the subjective aspect of institutions, i.e. to the means employed and to the ends pursued by actors, and in general, to action. Carrying out an objective study on the social structure thus becomes more difficult, and it is advisable to take into account the contributions of European authors, such as Marshall, Pareto, Durkheim and Weber. In fact, these are the authors that Persons does consider in *The Structure of Social Action*.

In his comment on Parsons' article, Coleman (1990: 336) stresses the "functionalist fallacy." This Parsons would have revealed after his first period of productivity. It would consist in an author's in not specifying how the need for shared norms and values contributes to the creation of institutions. Parsons' would therefore have ignored the relation of interdependence between the actions of individuals and organizations, and consequently neglected to consider the complexity of social life. Alexander (1990) comments on Parsons' article from a different viewpoint. Firstly, he remarks that Parsons makes continuous reference there to actors' moral commitment as it is evidenced by their actions; secondly, as he argues, Parsons shows that the relation that actors establish between means and ends is normatively regulated, but he does not discuss how they combine their rational actions with symbolic meanings.

Camic's interpretative thesis (1987) that Parsons would have aimed at protecting his own scientific reputation by carefully choosing his reference sources, has been questioned by other commentators. Some of them have stressed Parsons' and Weber's intellectual relation with the institutionally established and utilitarian economic theories. In fact, Alexander and Sciortino (1998) remark that: a) Camic has not provided an explicit standard for assessing reputation; b) Parsons rejected the institutionalist school for reasons (namely, their confusion between an analytical and a concrete approach) which were different from those pointed out by Camic; c) his rejection of institutionally established economic theory preceded his drafting of *The Structure of Social Action*. According to Alexander and Sciortino, Weber's influence can better explain this rejection. As regards the text on Protestant ethics, Parsons knew this author very well since Weber had been at the center of his intellectual interests during his period of study in Heidelberg.

According to Camic, given his acceptance of the marginalist economic theory, Weber would have influenced Parsons' position in the debate of that period between institutionally established economists and those whose thinking was viewed as marginal. Furthermore, during the years in which he prepared and published *The Structure of Social Action* (1937), Parsons' interests would have been in line with those of the Harvard economists, especially

Schumpeter. In fact, during this time period, both Schumpeter and Parsons were focusing on the development of a more effective theory, and they had both come to similar conclusions. However, their conclusions were incompatible with those of institutionally recognized economists. The word "theory," according to Parsons, should neither mean an empirical generalization, nor a philosophical conception; rather, it is a pattern which comprises generalized concepts and abstractions. The latter aim at providing an analytical description and an explanation of economic developments, and both are based on empirically established knowledge (Camic 1991: xxi-xxxiii; 1997).

Parsons would not only have come to this conception of theory under the influence of Schumpeter, but would also have shared with him, and in general with Harvard economists, his intention to formulate a unitary theory. Such an intention was clearly opposed to the aims of institutionally established economists. As for young Parsons' relations to Weber's intellectual heritage, the German thinker represented an essential point of reference for him. In Camic's opinion, however, there were some important epistemological differences between these two authors (Camic 1987: 434–436). Parsons pursued a variety of theoretical interests. As Camic argues, this made Parsons' epistemology and sociology significantly different from the theories of Weber. In fact, Parsons would have aimed at formulating some scientifically fruitful conceptual patterns in a definitive and non-historically conditioned way, i.e. at increasingly approaching a unitary theory of society. Finally, he also sought to keep commonsense knowledge radically separate from sociological knowledge. Parsons' interpretation of Weber would therefore have been partial and distortive according to Camic.

Camic (1991; 2005) has reconstructed the period of the young Parsons' education and training. First, there were the years at Amherst College, and then the period spent at the London School of Economics (1924–1925) and at the University of Heidelberg, where Weber had taught (1925–1926). It is on the basis of this reconstruction and that of the subsequent writings by Parsons concerning the themes of democracy and Nazism, that Camic has maintained that he did not sufficiently understand the cultural crisis Germany was facing during those years. This limitation itself would have allowed him to theorize freely about the development of a unitary culture out of the conditions of modernity. However, as Camic also observed, the rise of the Nazi party in Germany later obliged him Parsons to revise his evaluation of that country as an appropriate cultural model for the United States.

In contrast to Camic, other interpreters have argued that there was clearly a thematic continuity between Weber and Parsons. Schluchter (1979: 12) mentions the theme of rationality in modern society and notes that it was shared by Weber and Parsons, regardless of the epistemological discontinuity in their thought (see also Alexander and Sciortino 1996). Uta Gerhardt (2005a; 2005b) has preferred to stress Parsons' continuous commitment to democratic systems. However, she also stresses the basic difference, in the 1930s, between the regressive fundamentalism in dictatorial Germany and the progressive pluralism of liberal democracy in the United States. Furthermore and also in contrast to Camic, Gerhardt observes an epistemological continuity between Weber and Parsons. In her view it is not only the case that *The Structure of Social Action* (1937), but also *The Social System* (1951), actually highlight Parsons' strict adherence to Weber's methodological program. Gerhardt recalls Parsons' choice in favor of voluntarism, his precisely formulated conceptual pattern, the principles of value freedom and cognitive objectivity in the social sciences, and consequently, his epistemological imperative to keep the analysis of social reality separate from its evaluation. The presence of these conceptual elements in Weber's conception of social action (a normative order and the non-randomness of ends) was a key issue for Parsons in his first book. It also continued to be so later. Gerhardt therefore argues for the thesis of thematic and epistemological continuity between Weber and Parsons.

THE QUESTION OF THE CONTINUITY OF PARSONS' THOUGHT WITH THE WORK OF WEBER AND DURKHEIM

One of the questions debated in the secondary literature is whether or not these themes were dealt with by Parsons in a way that was concordant with the thought of both Weber and Durkheim. Here, we wish to preliminarily mention Bourdieu's harsh assessment of *The Structure of Social Action.* He considers this work indicative of a merely theoretical method of inquiry (and this in a negative sense), to the effect that it is too distant from actors' practices. Parsons would, however, have chosen several works written by some renowned authors (Marx excluded). His aim would have been to extract from them some compilations that may perhaps be useful for educational purposes, but not others (Bourdieu, Wacquant 1992: 224 and note 11). Bourdieu therefore denies the scientific utility of Parsons' aims and does so using epistemological arguments. Critical remarks by other authors were of a philological, rather than an epistemological nature.

The debate concerning Parsons' faithfulness to the classical authors considered in *The Structure of Social Action* has been set in motion by several articles, many of which have been quite critical of Parsons' interpretation of Weber and Durkheim. As regards Durkheim, Pope and Johnson agree with Parsons in judging that, for Durkheim, the sharing of sentiments and beliefs is the presupposition of social solidarity (Pope and Johnson 1983: 690). They also argue that the interpretation formulated by Parsons includes several interpretative errors: Parsons claims that Durkheim's' actor is possessed of a rational attitude of Durkheim's actor however this claim is devoid of any textual foundation; Parsons privileges values, rather than social factors, as a cause of suicide; Parsons also erroneously identifies a "voluntaristic" element, that is to say, one of spontaneous choice, in behaviors, which, as Pope argues, are instead determined in Durkheim's thought by moral rules originating in society, and conceived of by him as a set of autonomous and compulsory forces. Durkheim cannot therefore be considered a theorist of action, in the sense in which Parsons intends this term (Pope 1973; 1975. See also Nisbet 1974: 50–51).

Cohen (1975) substantially agrees with Pope's critical remarks, but keeps his distance from him on certain issues, thus mitigating the dispute with Parsons. The voluntaristic or independent status of the individual in relation to society, particularly relevant for Parsons, is also a factor in Durkheim's thought; but, Durkheim also sheds light, albeit in a contradictory fashion, on the coercive nature of morality. In addition, according to Cohen (1975) and in contradistinction to Pope (1975), Durkheim's writings on moral education aim at making scientific contributions to sociology and are not intended to address questions of social philosophy. In their joint articles, Pope, Cohen, Hazelrigg (Pope, Cohen, Hazelrigg 1975a; 1975b) have formulated further critical remarks concerning Parsons' interpretation of Weber. In particular: a) Weber gave by far less importance to normative factors than Parsons claimed he did. b) Parsons' references to some passages in Weber's works are insufficient to prove his interpretative thesis. Sometimes, Weber's own text even disproves it. c) The similarities Parsons thinks he has found between his thought and Weber's are based on quotations, the sense of which is sometimes distorted because they are taken out of their context. Finally, d) Parsons neglects some important aspects of Weber's work which actually clash with his own interpretation of it. Similarly, regarding the convergence which Parsons claims exists between the thought of Weber and Durkheim as concerns a "voluntaristic" action theory, Pope, Cohen, Hazelrigg raise several objections.

These can be summarized as follows: a) Durkheim's functionalism is not compatible with Weber's methodological individualism. Each of these two scholars would have completely rejected the epistemological position of the other if he had known it. b) Weber placed less importance on the normative elements of action than did Durkheim, arguing instead the thesis that market behaviors can be explained by considering actors' interests rather than their normative orientation. c) Behavioral regularities are explained by Durkheim as an effect of the legitimacy of a shared normative system; by contrast to this, Weber explains them as also being the effect of coercion. d) The conceptions of tradition and the sacred are completely different in these two authors.

Parsons responded to these critical remarks as follows: a) Pope, Cohen and Hazelrigg have neglected to include Weber's and Durkheim's writings within a wider perspective, and have instead privileged an unfruitful (in Parsons' opinion) and literal interpretation of them. b) The motivations for actions were considered by Durkheim to be an element of collective consciousness. c) The voluntaristic aspect is present in Durkheim's thought not only as voluntary consensus concerning internalized norms, but also as autonomy of action (whether rational or non-rational) for those individuals who actively participate in the modern division of labor by symbolically interacting with one another. In this connection, Parsons refers to Durkheim's concept of dynamic density. d) The convergences between Weber and Durkheim can be captured by means of a conceptual pattern. In some respects, this conceptual pattern is different from those used by both authors, but it is also drawn from their works. And, it can lead to the formulation of a general theory of action on the condition that it is interpreted in a non-restrictive way. Convergence can be evaluated on the base of a criterion that stresses these aspects rather than those which are opposed to them. However, pointing out their divergences may also be useful. The question of whether one interpretive intention or another is most pronounced depends on the interests of the authors whom one is reading as well as those of their interpreters. It also depends on the cultural climate of the time in which their works were written (Parsons 1976; 2007: 443).

In defense of Parsons, it has been stated that a correct interpretation of *The Structure of Social Action* should consider not only the cultural climate in which it was produced, but also its theoretical fruitfulness. Having been influenced by Weber and Jaspers, Parsons developed a persistent interest in the human existential condition (Tiryakian 2005: 278–281). However, he would also have highlighted (to a greater degree than Weber) the normative (not merely instrumental) aspect of modernity (Alexander 1983a: 134–135). Moreover, some scholars seem to prefer to take into account the evolution of Parson's thought, in addition to considering its continuity. As Camic suggests, it is perhaps best to "examine the numerous episodes of Parsons' intellectual career," placing each of them in its own time and space, and bearing in mind that his thought was subject to the effects of this. We must therefore not impute too much to the influence which Weber exerted on Parsons during the Heidelberg period (Camic 2005: 242–243; see also 1990b: 458). Similarly, Gerhardt reminds us that Parsons' work covers five decades, but his interest in Weber remained constant throughout this period (Gerhardt 2005b: 209).

The aforementioned critical remarks by Pope, Cohen and Hazelrigg, as well as Wrong's (1961) criticism, produced responses from Parsons himself and from some of his interpreters. According to Wrong, he may have given too much weight to the aspects of society stability, conformity and integration at the expense of individual autonomy. Parsons explicitly refers to Durkheim's teaching, and maintains that, on condition that it is of the right kind and quantity, the socialization process forms an essential set of conditions for developing the maximum conditions for putting freedoms into practice and enjoying them. He therefore clearly assigns great importance to socialization, a fact which undermines the validity of Wrong's interpretation. Hence, it was intended in this way, Wrong's remark could not be construed as critical. However, socialization of the individual does not involve merely the passive adoption of the constitutive guidelines put forth by the social system. Rather, the personality system and the social system become interpenetrated through mechanisms of adaptation and internalization. (Parsons 2007: 426–428, 450). With this statement Parsons does seem to answer Wrong's objections. But he also seems to successfully answer those of other interpreters who have seen as operative in his thought a conception of the individual which does not allow for creativity and freedom from influences and conditioning by the social environment (see, for example, Alexander 1988: 279–281).

According to Uta Gerhardt, the critical remarks made by Pope, Cohen and Hazelrigg point to a misinterpretation of Parsons' actual intentions in so far as he considered himself to be an interpreter of Weber. Given the historical and political events that had marked this period of his work, it is clear that Parsons' underwent a process of intellectual evolution. Also, neither author, Weber nor Parsons himself, would have maintained that interests are the only motivation for economic action. They both clearly wished to create a space for the theoretical consideration of norms (Gerhardt 2005: 208–209). Like Gerhardt, Joas and Knoebl (2009: 50) also believe that Pope, Cohen and Hazelrigg have misinterpreted Parsons. Their criticism is different, however, as it concerns the thesis of a convergence between Weber and Durkheim. Parsons' thesis makes exclusive reference to the theory of action, so he would never have maintained that there was a complete convergence between these two authors. These remarks do not seem, however, to answer the objection put forth by Pope, Cohen and Hazelrigg, in particular, they do not address the fact that Weber did not assign to the normative elements of action the relevance which Parsons claimed he did. In addition and according to other interpreters, Parsons would not have insisted on retaining the connection, as initially established by Weber, between historical research and theoretical synthesis. If he had, Parsons' sociological theory would have not eclipsed history (Zaret 1980).

Furthermore, the epistemological assumptions underlying Parsons' sociology, be they related to a *voluntaristic theory of action* or to the notion of *functional interdependence* among the elements of a system, would not be consistent with Weber's assumptions (Treviño 2005). Finally, it has been also remarked that Parsons' solution to the problem of social order in terms of shared norms does not seem appropriate for several reasons. As a matter of fact, he seems not to have provided a consistent definition of social norm. Sometimes, he describes it as a course of action and other times as an ideal situation pattern. Nor are there clear indications as to how he conceived the relations of these norms to each other and to the culture to which they contribute. Parsons would also not have explained how ultimate ends are linked to shared norms; nor would he have made clear whether shared norms either make up the normative order, or merely ensure its stability (Sciortino 1998: 105, 120–122).

These are obviously divergent interpretations of his thought. On the one hand, there is the claim of theoretical continuity between Weber and Parsons, and, in general, the appropriateness of Parsons' formulation of the problem of social order; and on the other hand, there is the question of the epistemological foundation for, and the explanatory capacity of, Parsons' conceptual pattern. The latter is such that he intends it to be scientifically useful and yet also not subject to the limitations of space and time. A considerable amount of exegetical literature has been developed around each of these critical remarks. We can discuss it here only briefly. First of all, however, there is Parsons' voluntary omission of the work of Simmel. As noted, Parsons knew this author and held him in high esteem, but decided not include him among those whose thought he examined in *The Structure of Social Action*. For, he did not believe that Simmel's epistemological program could be included within the thesis he had developed of a "convergence" among the different classical sociological authors, and a move toward a unitary theory of social action (Alexander 1998: 104–116; Levine 1985: 118–124).

NORMS AND THE SOCIAL ORDER

According to several interpreters, Parsons believes that social order depends on shared norms. These give purposes and assign rules of conduct, and they are taken to be morally obligatory. The aforementioned critical remarks, according to which Parsons would have overestimated the importance of the integration of society, the importance of norms for social order, and the degree to which they are internalized by the actors, are frequent in the reception of Parsons' work. They occur most often in relation to his first two major works, *The Structure of Social Action* and *The Social System* (e.g. Rocher 1974: 166–167; for a review of these critical remarks and their evaluation, Holmwood 2006b: xxxi-xxxiii; Sciortino 1998: 103–105). These criticisms are also often accompanied by requests for a closer theoretical examination of his thought. In this paragraph we shall consider at least some of them.

First, there are those of a well-known disciple of Parsons, Harold Garfinkel. He observes, in keeping with his ethno-methodological perspective, that the social and normative order dealt with by Parsons can be analyzed only if one collects an enormous amount (a *plenum*, in Garfinkel's words) of empirical observations. Parsons would therefore not notice the order as it is continuously enforced and taken for granted by those who participate in everyday interactions. The actor and the social order constitute each other simultaneously, so it is incorrect to construe them as separate entities. However, the analysis and reconstruction of this implicit order requires concepts and methods of analysis different from those used by Parsons, and also different from those employed by the representatives of traditional sociology (Garfinkel 2002: 68, 95, 97, 136–139; see also Garfinkel 2008: 200–203, 227–228: Heritage 1984: 304–305; Rawls 2002: 22–30; 2008: 23–24).

Secondly, the solution which Parsons provides to the problem of social order necessarily produces empirically motivated objections. In both modern and pre-modern societies a shared normative order cannot be effective if class, territorial, ethnic, and religious divisions prevail; similarly for theoretical objections. Values, because of their ambiguous and changeable nature, can neither always be turned into well-established goals and norms, nor into behaviors that evidence conformity to them. Furthermore, in Parsons' thought, values are reified concepts, for he does not take into account the fact that social actors who share these values put them into practice in keeping with their own interpretations of them, and with the emotional impact they have on the actors (Collins 2004: 102). Charles Camic, who has studied Parsons' early production in greater depth than other commentators, cites a vast literature concerning his solution to the problem of social and normative order (Camic 1989: 84–86). This literature can only be discussed here partially. C. Wright Mills' harsh criticism to Parsons concerns not only the style of his writing (which he judged to be obscure and twisted), but also the contents (which he considered empty and purely banal) in *The Social System*.

His criticism focuses above all on Parsons' solution to the problem of social order. Mills argues that the legitimacy provided by norms and values originates only from those who hold power; and, consequently, a shared normative structure can only be the result of ideological manipulation. It evidences social inequality rather than consensus (Mills 1959). In this connection, Mills mentions the theme of ideological manipulation on the part of power groups, a topic he had tackled few years earlier in his essay on power elites (Mills 1956). Parsons had objected that power should not be viewed as a "zero-sum game," one in which benefits are obtained by some to the detriment of others. Instead, as he claimed, benefits are an essential resource for any organized society. This objection has not convinced those who believe Parsons did not face this problem squarely. Mills is concerned with the influence and power exerted in an uncontrolled manner by corporation managers (who, in his view, form a social class) over American society as a whole. Since he was to some extent a prisoner of the liberal ideology of the past centuries, Parsons would not have noticed that in today's world there is, as Mills maintains, new power elite, one which is heedless of traditional liberal values (Hacker 1961).

Bryan S. Turner has commented that Mills' criticism de-valued the shared elements of the theories of Parsons and Mills. Both authors then merely seem to share an interest in the theme of values, in a sociological explanation of social order, and in the relation between personality and social system (Turner 1986: 192–193). Rex (1961: 105–107) has also expressed some reservations about Parsons' formulation of a normative solution to the problem of social order. However, as compared to Mills and those who share his critical point of view, Rex's criticism is differently structured. It does not focus on Parsons' defending a *status quo* disguised as ideological neutrality, but instead on making social integration depend on the system of values. And, this, he argues, is unsatisfactory theoretically. However, Parsons' analysis does not actually take into account the disputes within social systems about power distribution, even assuming that social integration depends on the system of values. Other commentators also share Rex's dissatisfaction with this theoretical point.

According to Giddens (Giddens 1968: 268–270; 1979: 138; 1984: 30) and other interpreters (Holmwood 1996: 113–114; Maranini 1979: XVIII-XIX), Parsons overestimated the extent to which normative obligations are adopted by the members of a society, and underestimated the importance of coercion in maintaining social order. Parsons would not have formulated a theory of action that takes into account the fact that these members interact with others in a competent way, creating and recreating social order "from the bottom up." In contrast to Dahrendorf (1958), Giddens does not argue that Parsons has neglected conflict and sketched out a utopian social system with no basis in history, one in which consensus and social equilibrium naturally prevail. Rather, the social order outlined by Parsons can, as Giddens also remarks, be defined by an external observer who is indifferent as to which groups obtain power, and also as to how it has become legitimated, or how legitimate power relates to illegitimate power. In this sense, Parsons did not have sufficiently developed a theory of action. For, the specific characteristics which he attributes to action, e.g. its rationality and adequacy from the actor's point of view, would result from a pre-established and abstract theoretical pattern.

Giddens' criticism has, however, not fully convinced all of Parsons' interpreters. Holmwood argues that Parsons actually held that real social systems are far from being perfectly integrated, and power inequality is inherent to them. On the other hand, Holmwood also observes that it is difficult to imagine a stable social system without mutual trust and shared norms (Holmwood 2006a: xxxii-xxxiii). However, Giddens' critical comments seem to converge, at least partly, with those of other authors, even if they begin from divergent epistemological assumptions. We here discuss the remarks of Homans, Whyte and Berger. Homans takes as his starting point the assumptions which underlie behavioral theory. He therefore has an epistemological position which differs from those of both Parsons and Giddens. He does, however, share Giddens' strong dislike for functionalist explanations. These explanations, Homans (1964) argues, specifically in reference to Parsons, merely formulate general and abstract propositions. It is not possible to infer from them the reasons for the actual behaviors of social actors.

To this Homans adds that functionalist scholars themselves provide psychological explanations, which are themselves inconsistent with the functionalist perspective as it defines the social relations they are attempting to understand. So, in the end social action cannot really be explained by their theories. The same kind of criticism (i.e. that Parsons lacked an effective theory of action) can be found also in authors who do not identify themselves with his functionalist approach, but also do not share Homans' behavioral theory. Whyte (1981), for example, observes that Parsons' concepts and theoretical propositions do not clearly relate to actual behaviors of social actors, and clarifies this by providing some examples drawn from organization theory. Among these objections and critical remarks, some comments made by Berger (1977) deserve consideration for the reason that Parsons in his reply does explicitly work out his thinking on the problem of social order.

According to Berger, who refers in passing to Giddens' writings, in his mature years Parsons considered the problem of social order to be a matter of normative integration among the various and functionally differentiated subsystems, or "spheres," each of which had its own specificity. Though he declares himself in agreement with Berger on several issues, Parsons reaffirms that the problem of order can only be solved within the theoretical frame of the functionalist and systemic sociology. He states his agreement with Berger on the following points: First, his own conception of social action has changed. After the publication of *The Structure* of *Social Action*, his conception of economy as a particular subsystem in which a given economic orientation prevails, led to a conception of economic action as individual and economically-oriented. Secondly, an explanation of social order can be developed only with the aid of sociological theory, not by pleading either economic factors, or in general those that cannot be analytically defined in sociological terms.

However, according to Parsons, Berger would not have clearly understood that, in conjunction with the other subsystems, the economic subsystem forms a social system. It is characterized by mutual relations among the subsystems, regulated by generalized symbolic media, and relates to other systems. These conceptual patterns are theoretical and therefore not subject to empirical verification. In other writings, Parsons argues that the problem of order can be solved in sociological terms by analyzing the effects of the institutional-ized patterns of normative culture on the social system; and also by analyzing the interdependence between the cultural and the social subsystems. This is a theoretical problem, one which does not justify taking a stance in favor of compliance with the existing social order or its preservation. In Parsons' opinion, interpreting this theoretical problem in the way Berger proposed amounted to twisting his thought (Parsons 1961a: 350. See also Staubmann 2005: 173–174).

Instead, Parsons is concerned about the fact that his country, the United States, seems particularly vulnerable to the risk of anomy. It might result from the pursuit of individual interest at the expense of the collective good. The Protestant religious heritage, which proved formative to the American culture, could become a source of division rather than social integration and solidarity. The conflict between liberalist and fundamentalist tenden-cies within this heritage would itself be the cause of such an outcome (Par-sons 2007: 454–459. See also Bellah 2005). The distinction between social and systemic integration, one which Lockwood (1964) focuses upon in a frequently quoted article, is relevant to evaluating the validity of Parsons' thinking on this as well as that of his interpreters. Social integration requires the absence of conflict among actors. It is therefore synonymous with moral or normative integration. By contrast, systemic integration presupposes the absence of any conflict among the parties to a social system. Dahrendorf and Rex have criticized Parsons' explanation of social integration as occur-ring primarily among actors, but they have not considered the problems and strains resulting from insufficient integration in the social system. Yet, Par-sons examined this carefully.

In this connection, Gouldner (1959; 1970) remarks that Parsons' attention to the needs of the system, in so far as it is viewed as a set of interdependent elements, and to the strains resulting from an inadequate satisfaction of those needs, have led him to theorize that system instability is the result of such strains. However, Gouldner objects that there is no reason to believe that each part of the system contributes equally to overall systemic change, since the parts are themselves autonomous. A generalized theory of change should therefore carefully weigh the specific contribution made by each part. To this theoretical objection (1970; 1972), Gouldner adds an ideological one. Parsons' theory would have been subject to a number of influences. These would have shaped it conservatively, and would have led him to accept the existing social order without reservation. He therefore did not have to ask whether or not prevailing goals and values are freely chosen or imposed.

Parsons' conservativism would have had its origins not only in his privileged social origins, but also in his experience of Harvard's intellectual milieu. It was conservative and isolated from the problems and the sufferings that the economic crisis of the 1930's was causing to American society. Alexander (1983b: 290–291; 293–297, 490 note 30) objects to Gouldner, but also to Mills, that these opinions significantly impoverish the understanding of Parsons' thought. According to Alexander, in Parsons' work (and in the social sciences in general) some ideological elements can be found, but they do not invalidate the objectivity of the work. In contrast to other functionalist theorists, Parsons was completely aware of the limits of functionalism and he made an explicit effort to systematically relate the analytical level of the social system to other levels, such as the level of the actor.

Still other positions have been articulated on Parsons' solution to the problem of order. Buckley, for example, argues that the word "order" may have two different meanings for Parsons. First, it may indicate interdependent structures and processes, and so designate cultural alternatives and processes of social conflict, including deviant behaviors and cultural processes. Secondly, this word may indicate elements of the system which are in mutual and harmonious relation, and thus bring balance to it. Any significant innovation can upset this equilibrium and even destroy the system unless some mechanisms of social control intervene. Buckley objects that the term "order" in this sense is unacceptable. The social system cannot, in fact, be intended as a living organism. It continuously changes its internal structure even if retains an identity of its own. And, in contrast to this, an organism can persist as long as it keeps its structure in face of changes to its environment. Parsons' reference to the *functional imperatives* of the social system is therefore incorrect and misleading (Buckley 1967: 16–17, 23–31).

Parsons' concept of equilibrium has also elicited both explanatory comments (Alexander 1987: 46–48) and critical remarks. Some commentators have argued that he is mistaken in using this concept in reference to the social system. But, his error here may depend on several factors. In the first place, the social system is open. This concept is derived from thermodynamics and so can be applied only in the case of closed systems. Secondly, it is inappropriate to describing continuous processes (a system either is, or is not, in a state of equilibrium). Furthermore, the equilibrium of a social system neither implies nor demonstrates its integration. It is therefore neither a synonym of social order, nor does it is necessarily assume a "homeostatic" tendency to perpetuate itself, and so achieve equilibrium in the social system. Finally, Parsons defines this concept, as well as that of interdependence, arbitrarily. (Bailey 1984).

Parsons' treatment of the theme of social order has attracted the attention of the Italian scholar Addario. He remarks that Parsons formulates two different conceptions of society. The term "society" designates, first, an organized set of norms and roles, and secondly, a collectivity of interacting actors. These different conceptions of order would have consequences for the ways in which Parsons conceives of social integration. As an organized set of norms and rules, integration pertains to the symbolic system, but as a collectivity of actors, interaction implies a community of their motivations, and hence, the sharing of ultimate ends. In both cases, as Addario observes, integration is a feature of the social system; however, it is problematic because it is also an element of psychic systems. There is, in fact, a divergence between psychic systems and social system. It occurs when subjective intentions do not accord with the equilibrium of the social system as a whole, and therefore with social integration, i.e. affection and other symbolic interchange media are not sufficient for this purpose (Addario 1998; 1999: 77–79).

As mentioned, the thesis that there occurred a conceptual and theoretical convergence between Weber and Durkheim has been criticized as textually unreliable. Warner (1978) provides a well-balanced evaluation of this thesis and the debate that has followed it. He also suggests considering the problem of social order from another point of view. As Warner and other interpreter's remark, Parsons did focus exclusively upon the normative aspect of action. However, norms and values do not themselves provide sufficient orientation to action and cannot therefore be used to solve the problem of the "randomness of ends"; so, also, for the problem of social order (Warner 1978; see also Savage 1981: 91–127). Instead of focusing on the normative element, Warner proposes to attend to the cognitive aspect of action. This can be done, he claims, without subordinating it to the normative aspect. The cognitive aspect implies that an actor orients his action to the belief (well-grounded or groundless, empirical or transcendent) that some things (events, relations, etc.) actually do exist. Giving greater attention to the cognitive aspect of action allows for the formulation of a more satisfactory theory. It thus also shows that there was greater continuity with Weber's and Durkheim's theoretical traditions than many critics claim, and makes it possible to overcome any dualism between individual and society, ideas and interests.

PARSONS' CONCEPTUAL PATTERNS

On the question of whether or not Parsons' conceptual patterns do indeed have explanatory power, particularly the pattern-variables frame as they were originally formulated in *The Social System*, the secondary literature points to conflicting conclusions. This seems to reflect a basic ambiguity inherent in these patterns (see Camic 1989: 89–94). We here consider only those interpretations which cannot be considered groundless because they originate from misunderstandings (see Martindale 1971, who erroneously views Parsons as an epistemological nominalist; see also, in this connection, Alexander 1983: 292, 296, and 490, note 30; Holmwood 2006: xxxiii). Some positive evaluations are based on the claim that the pattern-variables frame would have allowed for better understanding the different modes of articulation between normative orders and social structures (e.g. markets, religious associations, political bureaucracies, etc.). In general, Parsons' conceptual patterns can lead to analytical clarity, improve the interpretative and defining capacity of social facts, help explain them in a unitary and unambiguous way, and open up new areas of investigation (see Bourricaud 1984: 79–81; Fox, Lidz, Bershady 2005: 9; Rocher 1974: 167).

These positive assessments are, however, opposed by a number of detailed negative comments. In the first place, Parsons' assumption that he can rely on this pattern to account for all individual needs and goals given a limited number of alternatives, or *functional imperatives*, cannot possibly be empirically grounded. That is, he excludes from sociological analysis those methodologies which offer alternatives to his *analytical realism*. These include traditions different from those developed by the classical authors he is responding to in *The Structure of Social Action*, conceptions of action, personality, social structure, and those causes of, and solutions to, the problem of order, that diverge from his own (Camic 1989: 95). A second objection addresses the concept itself of *functional imperative*, insofar as it is intended as the set of institutions and processes that are necessary for the survival of a society. In fact, Parsons neither clearly defines what kind of survival he has in mind, nor does he provide any sort of discussion of it (Buckley 1967: 23–31; Giddens 1984: 270–272; Morse 1961: 144–145).

Furthermore, while Parsons would use the classifying pattern to argue the thesis that social order has normative foundations, many of his interpreters object that this attempt has not been successful. Through his voluntaristic conception of action, he aims to go beyond, and even overcome, the dichotomy between an explanation of social order which centers on objective factors, and another based on subjective factors. Another objection makes it clear that Parsons' conceptual pattern serves only an analytical purpose.

Even though it is abstract, it has nonetheless been used as a description of a social order in which normative integration and social control prevail. In his thought, analytical categories coincide with the empirical, social-cultural reality (Alexander 1983b: 166–167, 224–230; Rex 1961: 88–89). A second objection is that Parsons' "taxonomic fervor" is scientifically sterile since it does not make it possible for theoretical hypotheses or propositions to take into account actors' ever-changing practices. Any sociological theories that might be derived from it would, therefore, have to be provisional in character (Bourdieu, Wacquant 1992: 161 and note 115; Gouldner 1972: 305–312).

One objection formulated by authors of different theoretical orientations is that the conceptual pattern-variables frame, with its simultaneous reference to the social, the cultural and the personality systems, is not readily applicable. They claim that the ambivalence and indefiniteness that characterizes the relation between action and culture is something Parsons did not sufficiently highlight. Furthermore, because it is too rigid and abstract in nature, this conceptual pattern is far removed from social reality. In other words, it is scientifically sterile because it is not able to provide causal explanations of specific and socially relevant events. Parsons' thought allows that the peculiarities of these events be arbitrarily re-introduced into the pattern itself. In particular, it is difficult to understand in what sense purposes can be imputed to abstract collectivities, e.g. social systems or societies, if he does not specify the ways in which individual goals are aggregated and contribute to the formation of collective goals. Again, Parsons provides no clarification on these questions. His work, in particular *The Structure of Social Action,* does not rest on philosophical grounds, and so does not clarify the problem of sense. In other words, it does not make clear how the individual and intersubjective understanding of one's lived experience, and of the subjectively intentioned sense of others, can develop or even be possible. But, it is through this understanding that the actor relates to the life world.

Similarly, the alternatives designated by the term *pattern variables* are not be clearly delineated. Are they intended to provide alternatives to values? To cultural orientations? To empirical structures? By the same token, Parsons did not clarify the relations among these pairs of alternatives; or provide a reason as to why this is a question of dichotomous alternatives instead of being a matter of the degrees in which a particular variable is empirically observed; he also does not make clear why he takes these alternatives to be exhaustive. Furthermore, the analogy that he draws between the personality and social systems, may be useful to a psychologist, but it, too, has been viewed by some commentators as a source of difficulties and confusion. This is because the conceptual category of *need dispositions* does not satisfactorily describe the complexity of individual personalities. Instead, it is based on an impoverished vision of them (Baert 1998: 53–54; Baldwin 1981; Black 1961: 281–288; Crespi 1998; Habermas 1981; Holmwood 1996: 126–127; Homans 1964: 312–313; Joas, Knoebl 2009: 74–75; Maranini 1979: X; Martindale 1971: 171–174; 1972: 782–783; Morse 1961: 145–152; Muzzetto 1997: 251–268; Rocher 1974: 164–167; Schutz 1940).

Parsons replied only to some of his critics. Many criticisms were, however, formulated after his death. Parsons' reply to Schutz examines the relation between life world and science world; he interprets the discontinuity observed by Schutz between these two worlds as a break, and stresses the diversity of their respective intentions as he understands them. Schutz aims to investigate the actor's subjectivity, hence his thought issues in a philosophy. Parsons, by contrast, wishes to draw on classical authors formulate a conceptual pattern that can prove scientifically useful. In his view, sociology and philosophy are separate, though interdependent, disciplines (Almondo 1998: 156–160; Muzzetto 1997: 259).

Parsons dwells particularly on Black's (1961) objections to the alternatives that the pattern-variables frame makes available. For Parsons, it is not a question of alternatives to be faced by real actors, but rather of alternatives formulated for theoretical purposes with respect to the different orientations of a plurality of actors who interact within the framework of action systems. These systems operate at different analytical levels and interrelate as they face functional problems individually; that is, they face them both internally (e.g. the need for stable relations among action units), and externally (the need for generalized relations between the system and its environments). Jointly considered, these functional needs can be conceptually formulated through the AGIL conceptual pattern, rather than through the pattern-variables frame.

However, as Parsons remarked, Black did not take into account the AGIL conceptual pattern as it was developed in 1953. It concerns the structure of the action systems, i.e. institutionalized or internalized patterns of cultural meanings, systemic goals, and individual motivations. In the processes of interchange between systems and environment, resources are generated and consumed, and media, e.g. money, circulate. These processes maintain their own equilibrium; and it changes as the action system does, namely, with the differentiation of the action systems into the personality, the social and the cultural systems. Mechanisms of integration and adaptation to the environment therefore become functionally necessary. Thus the AGIL pattern makes it possible to conceptually arrange and interpret the tendencies that have emerged in today's societies, especially in the American society (see Parsons 1961a: 323–348).

It has been objected that symbolic interchange media (power, influence, commitment to values) do not circulate in the same way that money does. This is, it has been remarked, a misleading metaphor. There are, in fact, no prices attached to these, and exchanged quantities are not precisely defined (Lidz 2000: 412–413). In addition, it does not take into account the decidedly symbolic and communicative character of interchange media. In contrast to money, power and the other interchange media that have no intrinsic value, their circulation is not institutionalized. In general, they are not subject to the same restrictions as is money. And, the use of power is such that its legitimacy is a necessary condition for creating consensus. Finally, influence and commitment to values differ from money and power because their lower level of institutionalization, and their lesser capacity for serving as an object of exchange and use. This means that these qualities must be connected to individuals. (Habermas 1987: 256–282; Joas, Knoebl 2009: 79–95; Lidz 2000: 412–413).

Black's critical remarks were both preceded and followed by criticisms expressed by still other scholars. Schutz and Habermas, in particular, refer to the richness and variety of meanings in the real world, a stance which stands in sharp contrast to Parsons' schematism. Focusing on the shared aspects of their criticism of Parsons, they argue that the cultural system is a complex symbolic structure rich in significance, and that action is oriented to a system of values, and so to the cultural system itself. Social reality cannot be theoretically captured within the conceptual pattern of the pattern-variables frame. In other words, there is and can actually be no action on the theory of action as Parsons formulated it. Action is instead deeply rooted in the symbolic life world, and it is there that the motivations of social actors take on significance.

Action is therefore necessarily subjective. It cannot be conceptually related to the institutions and the processes that are described and explained in abstracto, regardless of the actors' motivations. Pre-established conceptual patterns such as Parsons' pattern variables are a case in point. The reference to norms interacted by the actors are motivated by this, and so also their subjective point of view and life world. The critical remarks addressed to Parsons by Schutz and Habermas have been considered at least partially unjustified (see respectively Fitzhenry 1986; Sciulli, Gerstein 1985: 375–376). As commentators have noted (Alexander 1983b: 490, note 30; Fitzhenry 1986: 171–178; Holmwood 2006a: xli), if it is true that Parsons did not sufficiently consider the subjective aspect of action, then Habermas, whose criticism of Parsons is continuous with Schutz's, has developed a theoretical framework that, paradoxically, is influenced by the thought of Parsons himself insofar as the strain between action theory and system theory is concerned.

Furthermore, Holmwood remarks that the theoretical framework developed by Parsons, in particular, *The Structure of Social Action*, combines in non-contradictory way analytical categories which are antithetical to each other because they derive from the incompatible positivist and idealist traditions. His voluntaristic conception of social action is supposed to build a bridge between these two different traditions, but it is built at the cost of radically altering the theoretical systems from which the framework itself derives (Holmwood 1996: 39–40, 114–115). Finally, some interpreters consider Parsons' conceptual pattern and his explanation of social order as outlined here (normative integration and control) to be incompatible with a voluntaristic conception of action.

THE DEBATE CONCERNING THE THEORY OF ACTION

A general theory of action such as that formulated by Parsons from a functionalist perspective is inconsistent—it has been maintained—with an explanation in voluntaristic and subjective terms. By choosing the social system as a unit of analysis, he in fact abandons the social actor's point of view. He has produced a classifying pattern which makes it possible to both establish a theoretical relation between the actor and his situation, and to work out a solution to the problems that arise from the functional relations between systems and their environments. However, these functional relations are not identical, nor can they be reduced, to those existing between the actor and the situation given that they involve a reference to systemic environments external to the actor. This makes it impossible to actually talk about *voluntarism*. The conceptual scheme of the pattern-variables frame therefore has required that Parsons abandon his voluntaristic conception and also radically reformulate the general theory of action. But, if he had done this, then, the theory of action would no longer concern the actor's orientation to others; instead, it would reflect the objective situation in which action takes place.

According to some commentators, in his mature years, Parsons therefore maintained his original intention to formulate a general theory of action. However, his reformulation of it into an objective of theory of action involved giving up his original voluntaristic theoretical and epistemological position, e.g. that of *The Structure of Social Action* (Adriaansens 1979; Dawe 1978: 400–408; Joas, Knoebl 2009: 74–75; Savage 1981: 162–165). Other interpreters prefer to emphasize the continuity of Parsons' interest in a theory of action, and to de-emphasize the presence of new theoretical elements in his subsequent works. As Wenzel writes in his introduction to the 1939 manuscript *Actor, Situation and Normative Pattern*, Parsons pursues his interest in a theory of action, but re-formulates it in terms that anticipate subsequent works, e.g. the *Working Papers in the Theory of Action*. This new formulation takes into account the relations that pertain to actor, situation, goals and means, analyzes the relations of interdependence between the action and the personality systems, and shows the actor's fundamental modes of orientation based on his situation and using Parsons' normative models (Wenzel 1986: 41–58).

According to Alexander (1978; 1982: 112; 1983b: 20–44, 102–103; 1988: 194–195), Parsons sought to reconcile his voluntaristic conception of action, which takes the individual as the unit of analysis, with the existence of a normative, and hence collective, interest; he did so by introducing the distinction between individual in a real sense and individual in an analytical sense. The real, empirically existing actor, adopts or, internalizes those ideal elements which are external to him, such as norms, and so acts voluntaristically, namely, creatively and so as not to be subject to compulsion. Collective order has a super-individual feature. It has no empirical existence and can be only described analytically. In this case, the contingencies of the actors' situations are set aside, and through a process of abstraction, the ideal, or normative, elements of their actions are isolated. Alexander adds that some of Parsons' critics, e.g. Gouldner, Dahrendorf and Rex, have not understood that he viewed collective, or normative, order as an analytical category and not an empirical description. It is therefore not synonymous with equilibrium. In complex societies, norms and values refer in the ideal not to themselves, but only to specific institutional contexts. They may be internalized, but they do not determine action. Instead, action retains its voluntaristic nature.

According to Alexander, therefore, there is no contrast between this order and a voluntaristic conception of action. Conflating different analytical levels would have induced hostile interpreters of Parsons' theory, but possibly also sympathetic ones, to erroneously formulate interpretations that were too narrow, and to develop misguided evaluations of his assumptions and of the many analytical dimensions of his work. (Alexander 1983b: Appendix). As Alexander maintains, Parsons himself may have unintentionally contributed to this situation by confusing his interpreters in a variety of ways: a) By using misleading analogies between the conceptual frame of the pattern variables (which regulate individual action), and the generalized interchange theory (which is analytically located at a macro-social level); b) By combining the theme of morality, as a theoretical-conceptual assumption about social order, with the theme of morality, as an institutional element learned through socialization. The latter is empirical, whereas the former is not; c) By identifying theoretical assumptions with empirical problems. Actors' commitment to the observance of norms is the theoretical assumption that allows for the existence of institutions; it is, however, an empirical problem whether the social system is in a condition of equilibrium and stability. The constitutive elements of a unit act are theoretically assumed; whereas the way in which the necessary resources are distributed to the social system is an empirical problem (Alexander 1983b: 162–169, 219–232, 308–309; 1987: 90–91; 1988: 194–195. See in this connection also Sciulli, Gerstein 1985: 378–379).

The Parsonian concept of *voluntarism* lends itself to a number of divergent interpretations. It has also been considered inadequate and misleading (See Camic 1989: 89–94). However, Parsons' position on the Utilitarian tradition can help clarify this. He maintained that Utilitarianism was not compatible with an explanation of solidarity or social integration. Parsons' concept of a *societal community*, as developed in his late works, would not only be consistent with this explanation. It would better suit modern differentiated societies, in which complex and intertwined relations between communities promotes discussion, persuasion, the mutual exertion of influence, the rational view of knowledge and action, and, consequently, increases the possibility that democratic systems will endure.

Utilitarianism would, under such circumstances, be compatible with the normative regulation of action since it governs economic and social relations in general. Solidarity and trust, generalized to all subsystems of the social system would then become possible. The particular relations existing between representatives of the free professions and their clients effectively make this clears. As noted, since these relations are not regulated by market norms, and so do not depend exclusively upon economic factors, they cannot be included among the relations on which the orthodox economic theory focuses. Instead, they should be analyzed within the theoretical framework of action systems. The fact that Parsons rejected the institutionalist theory does not imply that he accepted the rival "orthodox" economic theory, the latter being based on Utilitarianism and marginalism. Nor did it imply that he accepted Marxist theory. In fact, Parsons judges "orthodox" theory to be based on non-realistic presuppositions, and so incapable of solving the problem of social order. In his view, the attention which the economist Marshall paid to an integrated system of values and his criticism of Utilitarianism constituted theoretical progress (Alexander 1983b: 16; Camic 1989: 82–89; Gerhardt 2002: 254–261; 2005: 225; Holmwood 2006a: xiv–xvii; 2006b; Holton, Turner 1986: 30–41; Levine 1985: 118–120; Mayhew 1981; 1990; Sciortino 2005; Smelser 2005: 31–32).

In this connection, Gould (2005) has observed that the "orthodox" theory does not assume a natural identity of interests (as does Parsons), but rather assumes that actors have perfect information at their disposal, information that is also reliable and complete. According to the "orthodox" theory, it is on such grounds that social order can be established. However, in the absence of institutionalized sanctions against opportunistic behavior, and hence, of social norms considered legitimate because they conform to values shared by the economic actors, cooperation and social order are fundamentally impossible. In fact, the actors, e.g., corporate managers, can force their individual interests to prevail over the company's interest, thus undermining the trust that partners and other actors (e.g., external investors) have in the company. The continuity of corporate operation can thus become endangered over the long run. Durkheim and Parsons both insist on including in a contract terms which may initially have viewed as external to it, i.e. those which are not accounted for on "orthodox" economic theory. Their insistence would then be justified.

THE RECEPTION OF PARSONS' WORK: ECONOMIC SOCIOLOGY

Parsons' attempt to formulate a conceptual pattern which can include and put into systematic relation economic and social action can be observed in several important works published during the 1950s. The so-called *Marshall Lectures*, delivered by Parsons at Cambridge in 1953, are the beginning of this phase of his development. There is a considerable amount of exegetical literature about these lectures. It concerns the themes which Parsons deals with there, the aims he pursued, the extent to which he succeeded in reaching them, the place they occupy within the larger body of his work, and their current theoretical relevance. Parsons' treatment of economic theory has attracted great attention, in particular the way he used it to develop his own sociological theory. The theme of the relation between economic and sociological theory was developed in substantially the same way here as in the *Working Papers in the Theory of Action* (written with Bales and Shils, also published in 1953). It is to Richard Svedberg's credit that he discovered the texts of these lectures in the Harvard University archives. In his introduction, Swedberg (1991) focuses on several points which Parsons there addressed: a) his criticism of institutionalists, who are unable to make distinguish between the disciplines of economics and sociology; b) his appreciation of neo-classical theory, which attempted to carve out a definite field of investigation for itself, and, finally, c) the relations between economic theory and social system theory.

Smelser (1991; 2005), who co-authored *Economy and Society* with Parsons, considered the *Marshall Lectures* to be imperfect and incomplete, both because they were excessively general, and because their exposition of Keynes' theory was insufficient. Smelser also analyzed the relation of continuity/discontinuity between this and other, subsequent works on economic sociology, on the one hand, and the previous *Marshall Lectures*, on the other. Among the elements of continuity that he identified are: a) the formulation of the AGIL conceptual pattern; b) the interpenetration of economic relations by both values and cultural elements in general; c) their institutional regulation; d) the theoretical-conceptual inclusion of the economic subsystem within the social system, and, to a still greater degree of generality, within action systems.

Among the elements of discontinuity are: a) the extension into *Economy and Society* of the conceptual pattern used in the *Marshall Lectures*. In the former, Parsons dealt in greater detail with the concepts of system and subsystem, and the mutual relations between them; b) market analysis from a sociological-institutional point of view, particularly as focused on the labor market; c) the relevance attributed to the processes of internalization and globalization of economic life, and the consequences of this for a possible common and generalized system of norms and values.

Etzioni (1991) reviews and assesses Parsons' objections to neo-classical economists. By assuming perfect competition, they often ignore the larger social context in which the market economy operates, in particular, the role played by the internalized values of those who participate in exchanges. Parsons, however, neglects to consider the relevance of power in economic relations. Smelser (1991) criticizes Parsons' interpretation of Keynes and the so-called Lausanne School" (Walras and Pareto), as it is worked out in this cycle of lectures. First, he notes that Parsons would have kept his examination of economy as a social subsystem at too high a level of generality. It would therefore not have been useful to economists. In the second case, Smelser took Parsons' interpretation of Keynes to be incomplete because he does not dwell on the topic of unemployment, nor does he note that this constitutes an innovation on Keynes' part. In fact, this was a central theoretical concern to him (Keynes). The theories that Parsons and Smelser (1957) subsequently developed involved a refinement of the notion of system and subsystem, more precise definitions of the interchanges that occur among subsystems, and finally, an interpretation and evaluation of neo-classical concepts in keeping with the perspective provided by Parsons' theory of action.

Ritzer (1991) compares reformulations of economic theory as they were worked out by Parsons and Etzioni, respectively. As Ritzer remarks, Parsons' (but not Etzioni's) reformulation is incompatible with the prevailing economic theory. For, only Parsons' would have aimed to bring economic theory back into a conceptual sociological pattern, which was previously taken to be extraneous to it. On the other hand, Parsons' theoretical attempt to integrate these anticipates a modern approach, one which unites and summarizes quite divergent theoretical approaches. Buxton (1991) underscores the fact that Parsons' criticism of Utilitarianism was, first and foremost, addressed to this philosophy's inability to solve the problem of social order. Similarly, with his criticism of Marx (whom he considered a Utilitarian thinker with a particular ideological orientation) Parsons rejected the thesis of the inevitability of class conflict. In his view, occupational groups were a source of order and stability, not the reverse. On the theory of systems that Parsons was developing in those years, economic phenomena can be studied from the point of view of their contribution to the social system. Economy therefore comes to be considered a subsystem of the social system. The *Marshall Lectures* have served not only to outline the boundaries between economy and sociology, but also to make possible an analysis of the theoretical relations between these disciplines.

In his joint examination of the *Marshall Lectures* and *Economy and Society* (co-authored with Smelser), Gould (1991) has observed that, in these works, Parsons' openness to Utilitarianism is surprising considering his previous assessment of it, i.e., his objections to the underlying assumptions of orthodox economic theory, in particular, atomism, positivism, and its inability to solve the problem of social order. In these works of economic sociology Parsons stated (according to Gould), the need to sociologically organize economic systems. Still, the attempt he makes do this did not prove successful because he did not actually reconstruct micro and macro-economic theory in sociological terms. In fact, instead of providing an explanation for them, he only developed an abstract conceptual apparatus. In his economic theory, Keynes formulated theoretical propositions which connect certain economic variables with one another. Parsons, however, does not make it clear either whether or how his conceptual apparatus can illustrate these propositions; nor does he show how Keynes' theory can be included within a more general theory of social systems, one which can explain phenomena that are external to the economy, such as political processes.

Holton (1991), too, reviews the *Marshall Lecture* in conjunction with *Economy and Society*. He centers on Parsons' argument that from a sociological ("analytical") point of view, economic life can be conceptually organized under the adaptive subsystem of the social system. Economists, Holton adds, have not, however, taken an interest in Parsons' formulations. In fact, the questions he raised were, from their point of view, not only unusual but irrelevant. Moreover, his presentation was formulated in a language which was obscure and excessively abstract; also, it ignored the diverse nature of mainstream economic theory, and neglected to account for economists' ideological and methodological orientations.

Currently, economists seem to show greater interest in extra-economic variables and in non-market oriented economic systems. However, there is still a tendency among them to subordinate the discipline of sociology to economics. This runs counter to Parsons' theoretical effort. On the whole, however, the scholars who participated in this debate showed an appreciation of Parsons' attempt to integrate economic and sociological theory. They remarked, however, that it could at most be considered an interesting attempt to provide a conceptual apparatus for understanding economics, but not a successful attempt to formulate theoretical propositions through which economic

phenomena could be explained. As noted, Parsons' attempt to integrate economic and sociological theories continued and was further deepened in the
work he co-authored with Smelser, *Economy and Society* (1956).

Among the less than abundant literature which specifically focused on this
work, we here mention Holton's essay (1986a). It complements Muench's introduction (1982: 799–806), and the remarks expressed by Smelser. The latter
seeks to identify the reasons for the limited interest this book attracted among
economists and sociologists (Smelser 2005: 33–34). Holton does not limit
himself to summarizing its contents, but rather focuses on each element of
the AGIL pattern. He does so in order to explore the questions it raised given
the knowledge available at the time the essay was written. In his conclusion,
Holton observes that when evaluating *Economy and Society* it is preferable
to consider the contribution of the AGIL pattern to an economic sociology of
social change, rather than over against Veblen's institutionalism or Polanyi's
economic anthropology.

According to Holton, institutionalized economics did not have a theoretical orientation or developmental trajectory of its own. This would therefore
explain Parsons' limited interest in it. By contrast, however, Polanyi's work
does have these characteristics. It differs from Parsons' and Smelser's, however, insofar it lacks as any explanation in terms of historically indetermi-
nate, general relations between economy and society, Evolutionary theories
of change, by contrast, do attempt to account for this. It also differs insofar
as it is closed off from conventional economic theory, a theory that is not
anthropologically informed. On the other hand, through their category of the
social system Parsons and Smelser formulate a conceptual apparatus, which
is incompatible with Polanyi's conceptual relativism. Still, even this has not
been judged fruitful by economists, if their reviews of *Economy and Society*
are any indication. Quite often, the attempt to distinguish economic theory
from non-economic considerations has prevailed in their discourse. In any
case, there is still very limited communication between conventional economic theorists and economic sociologists, and Parsons' and Smelser's book
has not proved useful in bridging this gap. On the other hand, scholars who
have competencies and orientations differing from those of economists have
taken up dialogue with Parsons. Habermas is a case in point.

THE RECEPTION OF PARSONS' WORK:
SOCIETAL COMMUNITY

The connected but opposed themes of Utilitarianism and *societal community*
can be found in works from different periods of Parsons' production. Still,

there are some links among them. Some of his interpreters have connected the concept of *societal community* to other concepts now more frequently used, e.g. that of social capital. Parsons would have however given greater attention to social solidarity than to social integration; and to processes of differentiation rather than those of segmentation (Sciortino 2005: 119–121). A *societal community* implies the existence of a normative order based on a plurality of religious, political and economic factors (Alexander 1983b: 99), and it assumes the non-randomness of the ends which the actors set for themselves. In Weberian (and therefore not Parsonian) terms, a "societal community" requires that substantive rationality prevail (Peukert 2004: 1012–1013). On the other hand, if one accepts Utilitarianism, one does so on the assumption that actors' conduct is goal-oriented and that formal rationality characterizes society as a whole.

However, commentators have noted that the concept of "societal community" is ambiguously defined and that it seems to have been constructed by Parsons inconsistently. Indeed, the moral, cultural and political integration of some individuals or groups assumes the exclusion of others and the potential exercise of repression and coercion over them (Alexander 2005). This would not happen if subsystems did not interpenetrate each other, or if they were not functionally differentiated and connected with one another through generalized interchange media, and did not nevertheless maintain individual identities at the same time as they produced greater development in the subsystems and in the system as a whole (Muench 1981; 1982; 1990. As for the Parsons' interpretation provided by Muench, see Habermas 1987: 294–299; Sciulli, Gerstein 1985: 376–378). Concerning the notion of generalized media of interchange, some Parsons interpreters have considered it a very fruitful contribution to the development of the theory of action (Muench 1982: 804); others have judged it potentially ambiguous and misleading (Mayhew 1990: 302–304).

The generalized symbolic media of interchange, e.g. influence, persuasion and generalization of values, would, in Parsons' opinion, and also according to one interpretative line of thought (Wenzel 2005: 76), involve "a pluralism of solidarities" and a type of systemic trust that do not require rigid consensus on shared values. Their internal consistency and the possibility of mutual communication ensured by it would be sufficient (Wenzel 2005). Voluntaristic social action can lead to the creation of a community. The latter establishes and maintains itself thanks to the shared normative obligations and voluntarily commitment of participants (Tiryakian 1975: 28–30). One meaning of *societal community*, i.e. the *collegial form of organization*, has been judged by David Sciulli to be more suited to providing a theoretical solution to the problem of integration and social order.

This alternative to bureaucratic and democratic organization would allow the individuals who practice a profession, especially an academic one, to participate in collective solidarity. They could look out for their own interests at the same time as they protected those of the organization as a whole, and also limiting individuals' affective attachment to procedural norms and to those collectivities to which they belong. In this way, the *collegial form of organization* contributes to the formation of the moral order and ensures the cohesion of the social system. Members of a profession avail themselves of institutionalized procedures for this purpose. It is through these procedures that the arbitrary exercise of power is restricted and the social responsibility associated with a professional activity is normatively regulated. The action of professionals is determined by norms and values and is "voluntaristic" in this sense. Neither hierarchical subordination, as it develops in a bureaucratic organization, nor goal-oriented rationality, which prevails in a system of market exchanges, would predominate in this case (see in this connection, besides Parsons 1977: 218–220: Almondo 1998: 164–181; LaValle 1998: 196–199; Sciulli 1984: 534–536; 1986: 748, 753–754; 1990: 375–385).

Parsons' thesis that the value of cognitive rationality has a notable position in academic life has been considered less than tenable by Alexander. As he observes, it is an institutionalized value, which has never been fully accepted and continuously maintained. Holding to such a value assumes the existence of collective governmental bodies which are free from external interference. Under such conditions, this value is limited in its application by the ideological and subtly political activities that actually go on in universities. This often turns out to be the case even when these institutions freely pursue knowledge, which is their stated purpose. The academic world is subject to political and cultural pressures both external and internal, especially in periods of moral and political conflict. On the other hand, if the university seeks to maintain a position of neutrality in circumstances where ethical decisions have to be made, e.g. whether to take a stand against racism and anti-Semitism, this can undermine its moral authority (Alexander 1988: 175–189).

THE RECEPTION OF PARSONS' WORK IN HIS LAST PERIOD: SOCIAL EVOLUTION AND THE HUMAN CONDITION

Under certain conditions, voluntaristic action would be compatible with the creation of communities and organizations in modern society, and, in general, with its adaptive upgrading. Parsons' reflections on sociology would lead us to conclude that structural pluralism and individual freedom ensue from historical-social evolution. Those scholars whose thought is akin to

Parsons' functionalist-evolutionism have despite some reservations, shown themselves to be in favor of this theory of social change; other scholars have been highly critical of it. Those who take the functionalist approach explain change in terms of structural differentiation, generalization of the system of values, improved adaptation to environment; and therefore also in terms of progress in systemic evolution. It has been argued that a theory of structural differentiation would have to be based on three assumptions: a) that there is a tendency to ever higher levels of specialization in different functional areas; b) that there is a need on the part of the social system to achieve a higher level of adaptation to its environment. This explains the tendency to social change in the direction of more functionally specialized structures; and c) that the system or subsystem has the capacity to undergo adaptive upgrading if these structures are institutionalized (Colomy 1990: 466–468).

According to Muench and Schluchter, a prerequisite for evolution consists in a change in a society's value system. This allows the action system to better conform to its environment. Parsons himself would have explored this causal connection between cultural and social change (Muench 1982: 803–805; Schluchter 1979: 11, 26–27). Luhmann is perhaps the best-known of the theorists of social change who have adopted the evolutionary conception of social change. His response to Parsons is, however, ambivalent in some respects and reflects the complex relation between these two authors. Luhmann, like Parsons and functionalist scholars in general, conceives of change in terms of differentiation and evolution. He considers Parsons an eminent representative of this theory of change and of the sociological theory in general. Also, in his view, the processes of differentiation and inclusion (e.g. of the economic and political subsystems) can, as Parsons maintained, actually improve the social system's ability (or that of one of its subsystems) to adapt to the environment and bring about changes in the social structure.

However, Luhmann also raises some objections to Parsons' thesis that particular *evolutionary universals* are required to reach further stages of social evolution. First of all, he objects that there is no indication as to how systems can be harmonized with those of their environments with maximum effectiveness, given their growing differentiation and complexity. Normative integration, which according to Parsons is the necessary condition of the stability of the social order, can be achieved, in Luhmann's opinion, in a functionally differentiated society only under certain conditions, namely, if relations among subsystems are suitable to preserving the continuity of that society in relation to its external environment.

Furthermore, as Luhmann writes, the primacy which Parsons attributed to the concept of *structure* (as compared to *function* and *system*), leaves some theoretical questions unsolved. Among these questions are the possibilities of change and conflict, the ways in which these processes take place, and the relation between action theory and system theory. Concerning the concept of structure, it is an open question whether this concept is formulated for purely analytical purposes only or drawn from social reality for purposes of empirical description. Finally, before Parsons formulated his theory, evolutionary explanations of change had already been developed by some classical authors, such as Marx and Weber. They add nothing new if they are formulated in purely abstract terms (Luhmann 1970a: 106, 112, notes 41 and 42; 1970b: 113–115, 130–131, notes 1 and 2, 134–135, notes 41, 45, 49, 157, note 30; 1970c: 173, note 20; 1970d: 160, 168, notes 42, 47; 1990: 422–424. See also Wenzel 1986: 10–13).

Parsons' concept of *double contingency* attracted Luhmann's attention because it has considerable theoretical implications. According to Parsons, it applies to any interaction which occurs in stable social systems. In such systems, participants orient their institutionalized expectations for conduct and their actions not only according to their own motivations and interests, but also according to their interpretations of the other participants' behaviors and actions. They expect that their actions will be reciprocated, in compliance with those social norms that are in force and with values which are shared. Shared values regulate this system of social relations, and are therefore conducive to its integration. Thus, Luhmann observes that in modern, complex and differentiated societies, the double contingency of interactions assumes a type of social integration that is to be construed not as solidarity among individuals but as an evolutionary achievement of the social system. Integration is a property of the system, but not of the interactions among individuals, even though they are aware that expectations of institutionalized reciprocity are in place. These expectations promote the development of social systems (Parsons 1951: 36–45; Parsons, Bales and Shils 1953: 35–45; Luhmann 1987: 121, 129, note 36. On Luhmann's reading of Parsons, see Prandini 1998: 37–41; Sciulli, Gerstein 1985: 380; Vanderstraeten 2002).

Parsons' explanation of change in terms of structural differentiation and systemic evolution provided has occasioned still further comments and evaluations, mainly of a critical nature. These have been also expressed by scholars whose thought places them in a relation of theoretical continuity with Parsons' functionalism and who have a stated appreciation of his sociological analysis. In the late 1960s, for example, Nisbet, who considered Parsons an eminent theorist among contemporary sociologists (Nisbet 1969: 239), was still very critical of his formulation of a functionalist-evolutionary explanation, or conceptualization, of social change. He argued that Parsons' conceptual framework was so abstract that it would scarcely conform to the description of a real process of change as it occurs in a particular age or society. The cases he presents for explanatory purposes are elements of a classificatory pattern of change and do not contribute to explaining it. The causes, sources, conditions, and circumstances of change can be identified only through empirical analyses of real cases (Nisbet 1969: 262–267, and in general 251–304).

Though Eisenstadt mentions Parsons as one of the authors to whom he refers, (1964 a; 1964b), he remarks that: a) Social change neither necessarily produces the institutionalization of social and symbolic systems, nor does it set in motion a process of structural differentiation of these systems; b) The institutionalization of a social system does not involve full acceptance of norms and values by the groups placed inside it (classes, elites, sects); c) The process of institutionalization creates new collectivities and organization;. it therefore also generates new interests and orientations that may prove to be incompatible with those already in place within the institutions. The result can be conflict instead of integration. The descriptive and explanatory power of concepts, such as differentiation, institutionalization and social evolution, is therefore limited.

Alexander (1998: 211–212, 219, 223–228) considers Parsons' analytical distinction between the social, cultural, and personality systems to be an important contribution. A similar appreciation is shown for Parsons' view of these systems as autonomous and mutually interpenetrating; and also for his formulation and treatment of the concept of societal community. However, Alexander believes that Parsons has paid insufficient attention to the peculiarities of the cultural system (Alexander 1988: 220–221), and accepts Eisenstadt's criticism of Parsons' analysis of social change (Alexander 1988: 195–204). Like Eisenstadt, he holds that Parsons' explanation of change involves theoretical difficulties. They result from the use of concepts belonging to functionalist-evolutionary theory as it is used to analyze shifts in modern society. Cases in point would be the concepts of differentiation, adaptation to environment, and increased ability to solve those problems, social problems in particular, which originate from the external environment. Alexander objects that Parsons' optimistic vision of change projects an idealized image of the United States. It ignores, or would not be able to explain, tensions, conflicts, dramatic historic events and processes that occurred throughout the 20th century. Furthermore, there are important historical and national differences, which Parsons' modernization theory has not investigated (Alexander 1987: 80–81; 1992: 187–194; 2003: 197–200, 261 and note 5).

Other authors, whose thought is not at all in line with Parsons, and who are especially critical of his conceptual and theoretical formulations, have come to similar conclusions. Giddens is perhaps the most well-known of them. As he remarks, the concepts of adaptation and society, or culture, are vague and general. Also, for him the concept of evolution loses its significance when applied to non-biological phenomena. In addition, he believes that the evolutionist thought has highly limited explanatory power, and this for a number of reasons. In the first place, it views particular historical transitions as evolutionary stages to which general significance attaches. Secondly, it assumes that an analogy can be made between the development of the individual personality and socio-cultural development. Furthermore, it assumes that superiority in having any sort of power at one's disposal can be identified with the achievement of a higher stage of moral development. Finally, it also maintains that no historical change can occur in the absence of evolutionary processes.

According to Giddens, Parsons' argumentation exposes all of the typical faults of the functionalist-evolutionary thought. In particular, it presumes that the existing political and social order in the United States represents the highest stage of human evolutionary progress (Giddens 1984: 228–243, 270–274; see in this connection also Lidz 2005: 3328–330). Sanderson (2001: 438–439) replies that if the Parsonian concept of "adaptive capacity" is subject to these criticisms, then it ought to be applied in the analysis of individual choice rather than that of social development. The functionalist-evolutionary theory would then not be susceptible to these criticisms. In this connection, notable also are some remarks by Savage and Granovetter. Savage keeps his distance from some Parsons scholars, such as Gouldner, Lockwood and Dahrendorf, according to whom Parsons did not deal with the theme of social change. For Savage, however, such a criticism is textually groundless.

Nevertheless, according to Savage, the theory of change formulated by Parsons in structural-functionalist terms is unsatisfactory, because it is incomplete. It leaves the functioning mechanisms of a social system actually unidentified. It is also arbitrary, since cultural factors are placed in the highest position in the Parsonian control hierarchy, yet he does not provide an argument for this. This is therefore purely speculative. (Savage 1981: 196–233). Granovetter (1979; 1982) also criticizes various evolutionary theories of change, including Parsons'. He argues that they arrange societies in a hierarchical order, according to their assumed efficiency in solving problems posed by their environment, especially by the natural and social environment. In keeping with such theories, improved capacity for adaptation to present and future changes in their environment would result from this kind of efficiency. In Granovetter's opinion, however, a hierarchical arrangement of different societies according to this relative efficiency standard would be impracticable.

For, this arrangement would involve a comparison between the collective perceptions of production-related costs and the potential benefits thereof. But, the advantages to be gained from a comparison between costs and benefits accrue to individuals and cannot therefore be compared to one another. Furthermore, the levels of evolutionary development achieved by different societies, (which, for Parsons are units of analysis), cannot be separated theoretically because they are subject to mutual influences. Classifying and comparing different levels of environmental adaptation, and hence also of development in individual societies is therefore an arbitrary and meaningless exercise.

According to Parsons and other theorists of evolutionary change, social differentiation would be the necessary (though not sufficient), condition on which a society's could come to possess the capacity to adapt to its environment. As Granovetter notes (1979: 500–501), however, this argument does not take into consideration the fact that social differentiation can paradoxically reduce the adaptive capacity of a society, when a strong integration of that society with its environment results from differentiation. Not social differentiation, as Parsons would claim, would therefore indicate its degree of evolutionary progress; but rather a system's capacity to solve its problems of adaptation to the environment (Granovetter 1982: 947). Granovetter's criticism to the evolutionist theory has, however, not been universally accepted. It might be appropriate if were addressed only to the classificatory schemes used by Parsons. But, it cannot address the problem of the standards which evolutionist authors use for the purpose of distinguishing among societies according to their degree of "evolution" (see Nolan 1982: 943, note 1).

The concepts of the *human condition* and of *adaptive upgrading* are relevant only to works from Parsons' third and last period (see Lidz 2005). In their evaluation of their theoretical import, some interpreters have focused on the differentiation process and on its conceptual opposite, namely, de-differentiation. Parsons dealt with the latter on several occasions, for example, in his examination of McCarthyism. It is exemplified by fundamentalist tendencies and movements in the political, ethical, religious, and cultural field. It has been suggested that a joint consideration of these opposite processes would be necessary to better understand social change and the human condition in this age of globalization. For globalization implies uncertainty at the local level, but also point to the need for integration at the global level (Joas, Knoebl 2009: 90–91; Lechner 1990; Tiryakian 1992; 2005).

Assessment of Parsons' late works has not been unanimous. Some commentators who are critical of his style of theorizing have expressed the following remarks:

a. Parsons offers a description of social change but not an explanation of it, as he does not indicate its specific causes.
b. Conceiving of change in terms of adaptive upgrading presupposes an implicit ideological judgment about the general superiority of capitalist

societies, such as the United States. This country is considered more differentiated than any other, and therefore most adapted and "evolved" in relation to its environment (concerning these two points, the last of which recurs frequently, in particular among critics of a Marxist orientation, see Alexander and Colomy 1998: 53–55; Holmwood 1996: 94–95).

c. Parsons claims that the evolutionary change process involves new opportunities for inclusion and social-cultural integration. However, the empirical references he makes to particular contemporary societies, as the United States and Japan, raise the question of whether the conceptual categories he makes use of in describing and explaining change can be applied also in the analysis of change in societies, cultures and ages other than these (Alexander 1995: 14; Prandini 1998: 87–88).

d. In his explanation of change, Parsons does not dwell on tensions, economic crises, wars and totalitarianisms; instead, he provides an overly optimistic vision of both past and present (Alexander 1988: 62–66). In Habermas' assessment, he is insensitive to the possibility that citizens may be pushed "into the peripheral role of mere organization members," passively enjoying "paternalistically dispensed rights" (Habermas 1996: 78–79).

e. The conceptual overlap between cultural and social or systemic integration, Parsons shares with some of his critics such as Giddens, diminishes one's appreciation not only of cultural differences in little differentiated societies, but also of the mutual relations between the cultural and social systems. It is not scientifically advisable to limit oneself to arguing, as Parsons and other scholars have done, that social actors are restrained with respect to their actions by a shared culture. Its internal consistency of which should not be overestimated, nor the autonomy and interdependence of its constitutive elements, nor the ambiguities and discontinuities to which it is subject. In fact, a different causal connection can pertain. Cultural change may occur because social change occurs. It is also possible that cultural and social systems can vary independently of one another. Furthermore, the overlap between different analytical levels, i.e. between action (and life world) integration and social system integration, prevents the study of the formation of consensus and of the symbolic reproduction of society, namely, of shared beliefs, values and practices, by those who participate in the life world (Archer 1985; 2005; Habermas 1987: 153–155, 172–174, 232–234, 247–249, 283–285).

f. The orientation towards increasingly general and abstract values, in so far as it aims at evolutionary change, may actually not be sufficient to produce such change. It is therefore necessary to steadily connect the psychic systems with the social system through the consideration of human emotions and sentiments (Addario 1998).

g. Parsons explains evolutionary change in terms of causes which are internal to the social system, and in terms of the concept of *strain* placed on its constitutive elements. This being the case, it is also necessary to provide specific indications as to what the limits are on these causal effects and their temporal determinations: Which actors have produced them? How, when, and under which conditions are these effects perceived? (DiTomaso 1982: 24–25; Emirbayer, Mische 1998: 965–966).

h. Freedom and control are intrinsically contradictory elements of Parsons' theory of social change. In fact, the predominance of one of these elements is considered detrimental to the other: systemic evolution is either hindered by excessive freedom (i.e., that which is no longer subject to institutional control), or by excessive control (i.e., that which is no longer subject to justificatory values) (Donati 1998: 259–263).

i. Parsons' analysis of the human condition makes use of an articulated conceptual apparatus, but still does not have a sociological character. Rather, it has a metaphysical and philosophical one (Habermas 1987: 250– 256; Turner 1998: 41).

But, some commentators have also favorably assessed Parsons' theoretical work. Merton (1957) focused on *The Social System* in particular and considered his thought to be a definite step toward the establishment of a methodical foundation of contemporary sociological theory (Merton 1957: 83). Other interpreters have indicated their appreciation for the significance of Parsons' contribution to contemporary sociological theory, in particular, the problem of social order. They have also commented favorably on his attempt to formulate a systematic, unitary and consistent conceptual scheme, one which would be applicable across the social sciences and undergirded by empirical verification; on the breadth and philosophical relevance of the issues he raised and dealt with; on the depth of his treatment of them; and, finally, on his synthesis of the various sociological traditions (Alexander 1987: 111, 238; Habermas 1987: 199–200; Rocher 1974: 163–164). His development of the *telic system*, in particular, indicates that the whole action system derives from an ultimate principle(s). It is, therefore, not merely a metaphysical category (religious or otherwise), but a sociologically relevant analytical one. (Lidz 2000: 419–420).

CONCLUDING REMARKS

This chapter has dealt with various aspects of the reception of Parsons' work. To begin with, the first two periods of his production (1928–1963) have been examined and commented on. Relevant to this is Camic's interpretative thesis, according to which Parsons' choice to consider only a few authors in his first work would have based on his intention to protect his own scientific reputation in a university environment. Such an environment was hostile to the school of institutionalized economics, and supportive of an abstract and theoretical approach to the social sciences. This interpretive thesis has, however, been disputed by other commentators. They have remarked that the reasons why Parsons did not approach institutionalist economics are not those which Camic has indicated. Instead, they can be traced to Weber's influence on Parsons, especially Weber's methodological program.

We have also considered the different objections formulated against Parsons' thesis, i.e., that the theories of Weber and Durkheim converge toward a unitary theory of social action. The thesis proves groundless because these two authors start from mutually incompatible epistemological assumptions. They have also worked out different conceptual apparatuses, and explain behavioral regularities differently. Parsons replies that their conceptions objectively assume a voluntaristic aspect and that a shared conceptual apparatus can be abstracted out of their works. Some commentators have also disputed the Parsonian thesis that social order depends on shared norms; that these norms provide goals and rules for behavior; and that they are taken to be morally binding obligations. Parsons may have placed too great a value on social integration, and he may have overestimated the importance of norms and the extent to which they are internalized, all the while attributing too limited import to factors of conflict. The term "social order," and others such as "equilibrium" and "integration," are, according to Parsons, used only for analytical purposes and do not imply any defense of the existing order.

Parsons' conceptual patterns have also stimulated a great deal of debate. Some favorable evaluations have stressed their scientific utility, and noted that they have introduced greater analytical clarity and provided for better interpretative and definitional capacity where social events are concerned; they also comment that they have made possible unitary and articulated explanation, and opened up new opportunities for conducting social research. Negative evaluations maintain that these conceptual patterns are, on the contrary, overly rigid, and that they therefore limit the questions that sociological theory is able to address, and the answers it is able to provide. In addition, there is the objection that the Parsonian concept of functional equilibrium is inadequately defined, and in general, that his conceptual apparatus cannot be used to defend the thesis that the social order has normative grounds. The theoretical relation between the voluntaristic and the normative conceptions of action has been debated as well. Several commentators have argued that Parsons did not sufficiently clarify whether or not these two conceptions are compatible; nor did he indicate whether or not he himself retained the voluntaristic conception of action also in the middle and later periods of his production.

Economists and sociologists have considered Parsons' economic sociology too abstract in the sense that it provides conceptual apparatuses rather than explanations of economic phenomena. Still, his attempt to integrate economic and sociological theory has generally been appreciated. The concept of *societal community*, which is particularly relevant in Parsons' latest works, was however, according to some interpreters, not properly defined. Social integration of particular individuals or groups implies the exclusion of others, unless the interpenetration of differentiated and interconnected subsystems with generalized exchange media reconciles the functional need to retain the identities of the constitutive elements and, at the same time, ensure the development of subsystems, and, in general, of the action system.

Similarly, numerous commentators have remarked that Parsons' contribution to a theory of social change as an effect of structural differentiation and systemic evolution would be unsatisfactory. It has been remarked that no explanation of this is forthcoming and perhaps cannot be in the in the absence of the details of how, by whom, why change has occurred. Moreover, it is a fact that change can take place in a traumatic way. The concept of adaptation is too vague to be useful for explanatory purposes and lends itself to ideological use. The analogy between the development of individual personalities and social-cultural development, and between cultural and social change, is also hardly tenable. In the social sciences, there is no empirical basis for distinguishing different levels of evolution. It is possible to shed light on the causes of historical and social change, and to provide other relevant information to describe and explain it, but this can be done only through the empirical analysis of real cases. Finally, the human condition is a metaphysical construction that cannot find legitimate use in the social sciences.

Bibliography

Addario, N. 1998. "Differenziazione della società e contingenza morale. Il problema dell'integrazione sociale nella modernità." In *Talcott Parsons*, edited by Gandini R., 206–230. Milano: Bruno Mondadori.

———. Addario, N. 1999. *Azione e condizione umana. Talcott Parsons teorico dell'azione e interprete della modernità.* Soveria Mannelli (CZ): Rubbettino.

Adriaansens, H.P.M. "The Conceptual Dilemma: Towards a Better Understanding of the Development in Parsonian Action Theory." In *British Journal of Sociology* (30, 1979): 5–24.

Alexander, J.C. 1978. "Formal and Substantial Rationality in the Work of Talcott Parsons." In *American Sociological Review* (43): 177–198.

———. Alexander, J.C. 1983a. *The Classical Attempt at Theoretical Synthesis: Max Weber.* London: Routledge & Kegan Paul.

———. Alexander, J.C. 1983b. *The Modern Reconstruction of Classical Thought: Talcott Parsons.* Berkeley: University of California Press.

———. Alexander, J.C. 1987. *Twenty Lectures. Sociological Theory since World War II.* New York: Columbia University Press.

———. Alexander, J.C. 1988. *Action and Its Environments.* New York: Columbia University Press.

———. Alexander. J.C. 1990. "Commentary: Structure, Value, Action." In *American Sociological Review* (55): 339–345.

———. Alexander, J.C. 1992. "Durkheim's Problem and Differentiation Theory Today." In *Social Change and Modernity*, edited by Haferkamp, H., Smelser N.J., 179–204. Berkeley: University of California Press.

———. Alexander, J.C. 1995. *Fin de Siècle Social Theory.* London: Verso.

———. Alexander, J.C. 1998. *Neofunctionalism and After.* Oxford: Blackwell.

———. Alexander, J.C., Colomy, P. 1998. "Neofunctionalism Today: Reconstructing a Theoretical Tradition." in Alexander J.C., *Neofunctionalism and After*, 53–91 Oxford: Blackwell.

———. Alexander, J.C., Sciortino, G. 1998. "On Choosing One's Intellectual Predecessors: The Reductionism of Camic's Treatment of Parsons and the Institutionalists." In Alexander J.C. *Neofunctionalism and After,* 117–146. Oxford: Blackwell.

———. Alexander, J.C. 2005. "Contradictions in the Societal Community: The Promise and Disappointment of Parsons' Concept." In *After Parsons,* edited by Fox R.C., Lidz V.M., and H.J. Bershady, 93–110. New York: Russell Sage Foundation.

Almondo, P. "Le professioni o della razionalizzazione: la tesi parsonsiana." In *Talcott Parsons,* edited by Grandini R., 152–181, Milano: Bruno Mondadori, 1998.

Archer, M.S. 1985. "The Myth of Cultural Integration." In *The British Journal of Sociology* (36): 333–353.

———. Archer, M.S. 2005. "Structure, Culture and Agency." In *The Blackwell Companion to the Sociology of Culture,* edited by Jacobs M.D. and Weiss Hanrahan N., 17–34, Oxford: Blackwell.

Baert, P. *Social Theory in the Twentieth Century.* Cambridge: Polity, 1998. Italian translation. *La teoria sociale contemporanea.* Bologna: Il Mulino, 2002.

Bailey, K. "Beyond Functionalism: Towards a Nonequilibrium Analysis of Complex Social Systems." In *The British Journal of Sociology* (35, 1984).: 1–15.

Baldwin, A.L. "The Parsonian Theory of Personality." In *The Social Theories of Talcott Parsons,* edited by Black M., 153–190. Englewood Cliffs, N.J.: Prentice Hall, 1961.

Bellah, R.N. "God, Nation, and Self in America: some Tensions between Parsons, and Bellah." In *After Parsons,* edited by Fox R.C., Lidz V.M., and Bershady H.J., 237–247. New York: Russell Sage Foundation, 2005.

Black, A. "Some Questions about Parsons' Theories." In *The Social Theories of Talcott Parsons* edited by Black A., 268–288. Englewood Cliffs, N.J.: Prentice Hall, 1961.

Bershady, H.J. "Affect in Social Life." In *After Parsons* edited by Fox R.C., Lidz V.M., and Bershady H.J., 83–90. New York: Russell Sage Foundation, 2005.

Bortolini, M. (ed.). "Elenco dei testi citati e Bibliografia ragionata della letteratura secondaria su Talcott Parsons." In *Talcott Parsons,* edited by Prandini R., 288–325. Milano: Bruno Mondatori, 1998.

Bourdieu P., Wacquant L.J.D. (eds). *An Invitation to Reflexive Sociology.* Chicago: The University of Chicago Press, 1992.

Bourricaud, F. *The Sociology of Talcott Parsons.* Chicago: The University of Chicago Press, 1981.

Bronfenbrenner, U. "Parsons' Theory of Identification" In *The Social Theories of Talcott Parsons,* edited by Black M., 191–213 Englewood Cliffs, N.J.: Prentice Hall, 1961.

Buckley, W. *Sociology and Modern System Theory.* Englewood Cliffs, N.J.: Prentice Hall, 1967.

Burger, T. "Talcott Parsons, the Problem of Order in Society, and the Program of Analytical Sociology." In *American Journal of Sociology* (83, 1977): 320–339.

Buxton, W. "The Marshall Lectures and Social Scientific Practice." In *Sociological Inquiry* (61, 1991): 81–88.

Camic, C. 1979. "The Utilitarians Revisited." In *American Journal of Sociology* (85): 516–550.

———. Camic, C. 1987. "The Making of a Method: A Historical Reinterpretation of the Early Parsons." In *American Sociological Review* (52): 421–439.

———. Camic, C. 1989. *"Structure* after 50 Years: The Anatomy of a Charter." In *American Journal of Sociology* (95): 38–107.

———. Camic, C. 1990a. "An Historical Prologue." In *American Sociological Review* (55): 313–345.

———. Camic, C. 1990b. "Interpreting *The Structure of Social Action*: A Note on Tiryakian." In *American Journal of Sociology.* (96): 455–59.

———. Camic, C. 1991. *Talcott Parsons: The Early Essays.* Chicago: University of Chicago Press (Edited, with an Introduction).

———. Camic, C. 1992. "Reputation and Predecessor Selection: Parsons and the Institutionalists." In *American Sociological Review* (57): 421–445.

———. Camic, C. 1997. "The Monist Call to Sociological Theory: A Comment on the Early Parsons." Toronto: Paper presented at the 92nd Annual Meeting of the American Sociological Association.

———. Camic, C. 2005. "From Amherst to Heidelberg: On the Origins of Parsons's Conception of Culture." In *After Parsons,* edited by Fox R.C., Lidz V.M., and Bershady H.J., 240–263. New York: Russell Sage Foundation.

Cohen, J. 1975. "Moral Freedom Through Understanding. Comment on Pope ASR, August, 1973." In *American Sociological Review* (40): 104–106.

———. Cohen J., Hazelrigg L.F., and Pope W. 1975a. "De-Parsonizing Weber. A Critique of Parsons' Interpretation of Weber's Sociology." In *American Sociological Review* (40): 229–241.

———. Cohen J., Hazelrigg L.F., and Pope W. 1975b. "Reply to Parsons." In *American Sociological Review* (40): 670–674.

Coleman, J.S. "Commentary: Social Institutions and Social Theory." In *American Sociological Review* (55, 1990.): 333–339.

Collins, R. *Interaction Ritual Chains.* Princeton, N.J.: Princeton University Press, 2004.

Colomy, P. "Conclusion." In *Differentiation Theory and Social Change,* edited by Alexander C., Colomy, P., 465–495 New York: Columbia University Press, 1990.

Crespi, F. "Azione e cultura: I limiti della teoria di Talcott Parsons." In *Talcott Parsons,* edited by Prandini R., 125–151. Milano: Bruno Mondadori, 1998.

Dahrendorf, R. "Out of Utopia: Toward a Reorientation of Sociological Analysis." In *American Journal of Sociology* (64, 1958).: 115–127.

Dawe, A. "Theories of Social Action." In Pp. 362–417, in *A History of Sociological Analysis,* edited by Bottomore T., Nisbet R. New York: Basic Books, 1978.

Devereux, E.C.. "Parsons' Sociological Theory." In *The Social Theories of Talcott Parsons,* edited by Black M.: 1–63. Englewood Cliffs, N.J.: Prentice Hall, 1961.

DiTomaso, N. " 'Sociological Reductionism' from Parsons to Althusser: Linking Action and Structure in Social Theory." In *American Sociological Review* (47, 1982): 14–28.

Dubin, R. "Parsons' Actor: Continuities in Social Theory." In *American Sociological Review* (25, 1960): 457–466.

Eisenstadt, S.N. 1964a. "Institutionalization and Social Change." In *American Sociological Review* (29): 235–247.

———. Eisenstadt, S.N. 1964b. "Social Change, Differentiation, and Evolution." In *American Sociological Review* (29): 375–386.

Emirbayer M., Mische A. "What is Agency?" In *American Journal of Sociology* (103, 1998): 962–1023.

Etzioni, A. "Socio-Economics Revisited." In *Sociological Inquiry* (61, 1991): 68–73.

Fitzhenry, R. "Parsons, Schutz and the Problem of *Verstehen*." In *Talcott Parsons on Economy and Society*, edited by Holton R.J. and Turner B., 143–178. London: Routledge, 1986.

Fox R.C., Lidz V.M., and Bershady H.J. "Introduction." In *After Parsons*, edited by Fox R.C., Lidz V.M., and Bershady H.J., 1–27. New York: Russell Sage Foundation, 2005.

Garfinkel, H. 2002. *Ethnomethodology's Program. Working out Durkheim's Aphorism* (A.W. Rawls ed.). Lanham, Maryland: Rowman & Littlefield.

———. Garfinkel, H. 2008. *Toward a Sociological Theory of Information* (A.W. Rawls ed.). London: Paradigm Publishers.

Gerhardt, U., 2002. *Talcott Parsons. An Intellectual Biography.* Cambridge: Cambridge University Press.

———. Gerhardt, U. 2005a. "Why Read *The Social System* Today? Three Reasons and a Plea." In *Journal of Classical Sociology* (5): 267–301.

———. Gerhardt, U. 2005b. "The Weberian Talcott Parsons: Sociological Theory in Three Decades of American History." In *After Parsons*, edited by Fox R.C., Lidz V.M., and Bershady H.J., 208–239. New York: Russell Sage Foundation.

Giddens, A. 1968. "Power in the Recent Writings of Talcott Parsons." In *Sociology* (2): 257–272.

———. Giddens, A. 1979. *Nuove regole del metodo sociologico.* Bologna: Il Mulino.

———. Giddens, A. 1984. *The Constitution of Society.* Cambridge: Polity.

Gould, M. "Looming Catastrophe: How and Why 'Law and Economics' Undermines Fiduciary Duties in Corporate Law." In *After Parsons*, edited by Fox R.C., Lidz V.M., and Bershady H.J., 44–65. New York: Russell Sage Foundation, 2005.

Gouldner, A. 1959. "Reciprocity and Antinomy in Functional Theory." In *Symposium on Sociological Theory*, edited by Gross L.Z., 241–270. Evanston: Harper & Row.

———. Gouldner, A. 1970. *The Coming Crisis of Western Sociology.* New York: Basic Books. Italian translation *La crisi della sociologia.* Bologna: Il Mulino, 1972.

Granovetter, M. 1979. "The Idea of 'Advancement' in Theories of Social Evolution and Development." In *American Journal of Sociology* (85): 489–515.

———. Granovetter, M. 1982. "Reply to Nolan." In *American Journal of Sociology* (88): 947–950.

Habermas, J. 1981. "Talcott Parsons: Problems of Theory Construction." In *Sociological Inquiry* (5)1. 173–196.

———. Habermas, J. 1987. *The Theory of Communicative Action. Lifeworld and Systems: A Critique of Functionalist Reason.* Boston: Beacon Press.

——. Habermas J. 1996b. *Between Facts and Norms.* Cambridge, UK: Polity Press.

Hacker, A. "Sociology and Ideology." In *The Social Theories of Talcott Parsons,* edited by Black A., 289–310. Englewood Cliffs, N.J.: Prentice Hall, 1961.

Hamilton, P. *Talcott Parsons.* Bologna: Il Mulino, 1989 (1983).

Heritage, J. C., *Garfinkel and Ethnomethodology,* Cambridge, Polity Press, 1984.

Holmwood, J. *Founding Sociology?: Talcott Parsons and the Idea of General Theory.* London: Longman, 1996.

——. Holmwood, J. 2006a. "Introduction." In *Talcott Parsons,* edited by Holmwood J., XII-LI.. London: Ashgate.

——. Holmwood, J. 2006b. "Economics, Sociology, and the Professional Complex: Talcott Parsons and the Critique of Orthodox Economics." In *The American Journal of Economics and Sociology* (65): 127–160.

Holton, R.J. 1986a. "Talcott Parsons and the Theory of Economy and Society." In *Talcott Parsons on Economy and Society,* edited by Holton R.J. and Turner B., 25–105. London: Routledge.

——. Holton, R.J. 1986b. "Parsons and His Critics: on the Ubiquity of Functionalism." In *Talcott Parsons on Economy and Society,* edited by Holton R.J. and Turner B., 179–206. London: Routledge.

——. Holton, R.J. 2001. "Talcott Parsons: Conservative Apologist or Irreplaceable Icon?" In *Handbook of Social Theory,* edited by Ritzer G., Smart B., 152–162. London: Sage.

——. Holton R.J., Turner B. 1986a. "Reading Talcott Parsons: Introductory Remarks." In *Talcott Parsons on Economy and Society,* edited by Holton R.J. and Turner B., 1–24. London: Routledge.

——. Holton R.J., Turner B. 1986b. "Against Nostalgia: Talcott Parsons and a Sociology for the Modern World." In *Talcott Parsons on Economy and Society,* edited by Holton R.J. and Turner B., 207–234. London: Routledge.

Homans, G. "Bringing Men Back In." In *American Sociological Review* (29, 1964): 809–818.

Joas, H., Knoebl W. *Social Theory. Twenty Introductory Lectures.* Cambridge: Cambridge University Press, 2009.

Johnson, B. *Functionalism in Modern Sociology: Understanding Talcott Parsons.* Morriston, N.J.: General Learning Press, 1975.

Landsberger, H.A. "Parsons' Theory of Organizations." In *The Social Theories of Talcott Parsons,* edited by Black M., 214–249. Englewood Cliffs, N.J.: Prentice Hall, 1961.

La Valle, D. "Talcott Parsons: cultura, sistema sociale e sviluppo economico." In *Talcott Parsons,* edited by Grandini R.,182–205. Milano: Bruno Mondadori, 1998.

Lechner, F.J. "Fundamentalism and Sociocultural Revitalization: On the Logic of De-differentiation." In *Differentiation Theory and Social Change,* edited by Alexander J.C., Colomy P., 88–118. New York: Columbia University Press, 1990.

Levine, D.N. 1985. *The Flight from Ambiguity.* Chicago, Ill.: The University of Chicago Press.

Levine, D.N. 2005. "Modernity and Its Endless Discontents." In *After Parsons,* edited by Fox R.C., Lidz V.M., and Bershady H.J., 148–165. New York: Russell Sage Foundation.

Lidz, V.M. 2000. "Talcott Parsons." In *The Blackwell Companion to Major Social Theorists,* edited by Ritzer G., 388–431. Oxford: Blackwell.

———. Lidz, V.M. 2005. "Social Evolution' in the Light of the Human-Condition Paradigm." In *After Parsons,* edited by Fox R.C., Lidz V.M., and Bershady H.J., 308–333. New York: Russell Sage Foundation.

Lockwood, D. 1964. "Social Integration and System Integration." In *Explorations in Social Change,* edited by Zollschan G.K. and Hirsch W., 244–257. London: Routledge & Kegan Paul.

Luhmann, N. 1970a. "Reflexive Mechanismen." In *Soziologische Aufklaerung* (Bd. 1), 92–112,. Opladen: Westdeuscher Verlag.

Luhmann, N. 1970b. "Soziologie als Theorie sozialer Systeme." In *Soziologische Aufklaerung* (Bd. 1), 113–136. Opladen: Weatdeuscher Verlag.

———. Luhmann, N. 1970c. "Soziologie des politischen Systems." In *Soziologische Aufklaerung* (Bd. 1), 137–177. Opladen: Westdeuscher Verlag.

———. Luhmann, N. 1970d. "Evolution und Geschichte." In *Soziologische Aufklaerung* (Bd. 2), 150–169. Opladen: Westdeuscher Verlag.

———. Luhmann, N. 1987. "The Evolutionary Differentiation between Society and Interaction." In *The Micro-Macro Link,* edited by Alexander J. C., Giesen B., Münch R. and Smelser N. J., 112–131, The University of California Press, Berkeley, CA.

———. Luhmann, N. 1990. "The Paradox of System Differentiation and the Evolution of Society." In *Differentiation Theory and Social Change*, edited by Alexander J.C., Colomy P., 409–440. New York: Columbia University Press.

Maranini, P. "Introduzione." In Parsons T. 1979 (1967). *Teoria sociologica e società moderna,* IX-XXI, Milano: Etas Libri, 1979.

Martindale, D. 1960. *The Nature and Types of Sociological Theory.* Boston: Houghton Mifflin. Italian translation: *Tipologia ed storia della teoria sociologica.* Bologna: Il Mulino, 1968.

———. Martindale, D. 1971. "Talcott Parsons' Theoretical Metamorphosis from Social Behaviorism to Macrofunctionalism." In *Institutions and Exchange: The Sociologies of Talcott Parsons and George Caspar Homans,* edited b Turk H., Simpson R.L., 165–174. New York: Bobbs Merril.

Mayhew, L. 1984. "In Defense of Modernity: Talcott Parsons and the Utilitarian Tradition." In *American Journal of Sociology* (89): 1273–1305.

———. Mayhew, L. 1990. "The Differentiation of the Solidary Public." In *Differentiation Theory and Social Change,* edited by Alexander J.C., Colomy P., 294–322. New York: Columbia University Press.

Merton, R.K. *Social Theory and Social Structure.* New York: The Free Press, 1957.

Mills Wright, C. 1956. *The Power Elites.* Oxford: Oxford University Press. Italian translation: *La élite del potere.* Milano: Feltrinelli, 1966.

———. Mills Wright, C. 1959(1968). *The Sociological Imagination.* Oxford: Oxford University Press. Italian translation: *L'immaginazione sociologica.* Milano: Il Saggiatore.

Morse, C. "The Functional Imperatives." In *The Social Theories of Talcott Parsons,* edited by Black M., 100–152. Englewood Cliffs, N.J.: Prentice Hall, 1961.

Muench, R. 1981. "Talcott Parsons and the Theory of Action: I. The Structure of the Kantian Core." In *American Journal of Sociology* (86): 709–739.

———. Muench, R. 1982. "Talcott Parsons and the Theory of Action. II: The Continuity of the Development." In *American Journal of Sociology* (87): 771–826.

———. Muench, R. 1987. "Parsonian Theory Today: In Search of a New Synthesis." In *Social Theory Today,* edited by Giddens A. and Turner J.H., 116–155. Cambridge: Polity Press.

———. Muench, R. 1990. "Differentiation, Rationalization, Interpenetration: The Emergence of Modern Society." In *Differentiation Theory and Social Change,* edited by Alexander J.C., Colomy P., 441–464. New York: Columbia University Press.

Nisbet, R.A. 1969. *Social Change and History.* New York: Oxford University Press.

———. Nisbet, R.A. 1974. *The Sociology of Emile Durkheim.* New York: Oxford University Press.

Nolan, P.D. "Energy, Information, and Sociocultural 'Advancement.' " In *American Journal of Sociology* (87, 1982): 942–946.

Parsons, T. 1928. "Capitalism in Recent German Literature: Sombart and Weber. I." In *Journal of Political Economy* (36): 641–661.

———. Parsons, T. 1929. "Capitalism in Recent German Literature: Sombart and Weber. II." In *Journal of Political Economy* (37): 31–51.

———. Parsons, T. 1934. "Society." Vol. 14: 225–231. In *Encyclopedia of the Social Sciences.* New York: MacMillan.

———. Parsons, T. 1949 (1937). *The Structure of Social Action.* New York: The Free Press.

———. Parsons, T. 1951. *The Social System.* New York: The Free Press.

———. Parsons, T. 1961a. "The Point of View of the Author." In *The Social Theories of Talcott Parsons,* edited by Black M., 311–363. Englewood Cliffs, N.J.: Prentice Hall.

———. Parsons, T. 1961b. "An Outline of the Social System." In *Theories of Society. Foundations of Modern Sociological Theory,* edited by Parsons T., Shils E., Naegele K.D. and Pitts J.R., 30–79. New York: The Free Press, 1965.

———. Parsons, T. 1964a. *Social Structure and Personality.* New York: The Free Press.

———. Parsons, T. 1964b. "Evolutionary Universals in Society." In *American Sociological Review* (29): 339–357.

———. Parsons, T. 1966. *Societies. Evolutionary and Comparative Perspectives.* London: Prentice-Hall.

———. Parsons, T. 1969a (1960). "Pattern Variables Revisited: A Response to Robert Dubin." In *Sociological Theory. An Introduction,* edited by Wallace W.L., 270–289. Chicago: Aldine.

———. Parsons, T. 1969b. *Politics and Social Structure.* New York: The Free Press.

———. Parsons, T. 1970. "On Building Social System Theory. A Personal History." In *Daedalus* (99): 826–81.

————. Parsons, T. 1971. *The System of Modern Societies.* London : Prentice-Hall.

————. Parsons, T. 1975. "Comment on 'Parsons' Interpretation of Durkheim' and on 'Moral Freedom through Understanding." In *American Sociological Review* (40): 106–111.

————. Parsons, T. 1976. "Reply to Cohen, Hazelrigg and Pope." In *American Sociological Review* (41:2): 361–365.

————. Parsons, T. 1977a. *Social Systems and the Evolution of Action Theory.* New York: The Free Press.

————. Parsons, T. 1977 b. "Comment on Burger's Critique." In *American Sociological Review* (83): 335–339.

————. Parsons, T. 1978. *Action Theory and the Human Condition.* New York: The Free Press.

————. Parsons, T. 1979 (1967). *Teoria sociologica e società moderna.* Milano: Etas Libri.

————. Parsons, T. 1986 (1939). *Aktor, Situation und normative Muster.* Frankfurt: Suhrkamp.

————. Parsons, T. 1990 (1934). "Prolegomena to a Theory of Social Institutions." In *American Sociological Review* (55): 319–39.

————. Parsons, T. 1991 (1953). "The Integration of Economic and Sociological Theory, The Marshall Lectures." In *Sociological Inquiry* (61): 10–59.

————. Parsons, T. 2007 (1979). *American Society. A Theory of the Societal Community* (G. Sciortino, ed.) London: Paradigm Publishers.

————. Parsons T., Bales R.F. and. Shils E.A. 1953. *Working Papers in the Theory of Action.* New York: The Free Press.

————. Parsons T., Platt G. 1973. *The American University.* Cambridge: Harvard University Press.

————. Parsons T. and Shils E.A. 2001 (1951). *Toward a General Theory of Action.* London: Transaction Publishers.

————. Parsons T. and Smelser N.J. 1957. *Economy and Society.* London: Routledge & Kegan Paul.

Peukert, H. "Max Weber: Precursor of Economic Sociology and Heterodox Economics?" In *The American Journal of Economics and Sociology* (63:5, 2004): 987–1020.

Pope, W. 1973. "Classic on Classic: Parsons' Interpretation of Durkheim." In *American Sociological Review* (38): 399–415.

————. Pope, W. 1975. "Parsons on Durkheim Revisited: Reply to Cohen and Parsons." In *American Sociological Review* (40): 111–115.

————. Pope, W., Johnson, B.D. 1983. "Inside Organic Solidarity." In *American Sociological Review* (48): 681–692.

————. Pope, W., Cohen, J. and Hazelrigg, L.F. 1975a. "On the Divergence of Weber and Durkheim: A Critique of Parsons' Convergence Thesis." In *American Sociological Review* (40): 417–427.

————. Pope, W., Cohen, J. and Hazelrigg, L.F. 1975b. "Reply to Parsons." In *American Sociological Review* (40): 670–674.

Prandini, R. "Talcott Parsons e la cultura della società." In *Talcott Parsons*, edited by Prandini R., 1–97. Milano: Bruno Mondatori, 1998.

Rawls, A.W. 2002. "Introduction." In Garfinkel H., *Ethnomethodology's Program. Working out Durkheim's Aphorism*, edited by Rawls A.W., 1–64. Lanham, Maryland: Rowman & Littlefield.

———. Rawls, A.W. 2008. "Editor's Introduction." In Garfinkel H., *Toward a Sociological Theory of Information*, edited by Rawls A.W., 1–100. London: Paradigm Publishers.

Rex, J. *Key Problems of Sociological Theory*. London: Routledge & Kegan Paul, 1961.

Ritzer, G. "Talcott Parsons' Marshall Lectures: Contemporary But Flawed." In *Sociological Inquiry* (61, 1991): 74–80.

Rocher, G. *Talcott Parsons and American Sociology*. London: Nelson, 1974 (1972).

Sanderson, S.K. "Evolutionary Theorizing." In *Handbook of Sociological Theory*, edited by Turner J.H., 435–455. New York: Springer, 2001.

Savage, S.P. *The Theories of Talcott Parsons*. New York: St. Martin's Press, 1981.

Schutz, A. "Parsons' Theory of Social Action." In *Talcott Parsons*, edited by Holmwood J., 47–92. London: Ashgate, 2006 (1940).

Sciortino, G. 1998. "Sul concetto di ordine normativo nella teoria dell'azione." In *Talcott Parsons*, edited by Prandini R., 98–124. Milano: Bruno Mondadori.

———. Sciortino, G. 2005. "How Different Can We Be? Parsons's Societal Community, Pluralism, and the Multicultural Debate." In *After Parsons*, edited by Fox R.C., Lidz V.M., and Bershady H.J., 111–136. New York: Russell Sage Foundation.

———. Sciortino, G. 2007. "Introduction: The Action of Social Structure." In Parsons T. (2007) (1979), *American Society. A Theory of the Societal Community*, edited by Sciortino G., 1–53. London: Paradigm Publishers.

Sciulli, D. 1984. "Talcott Parsons's Analytical Critique of Marxism's Concept of Alienation." In *American Journal of Sociology* (90): 514–540.

———. Sciulli D., Gerstein D. 1985. "Social Theory and Talcott Parsons in the 1980." In *Annual Review of Sociology* (11.): 369–387. Reprinted, with permission, from the Annual Review of Sociology, Vol. 11, ©1985 by Annual Reviews www.annualreviews.org.

———. Sciulli, D. 1986. "Voluntaristic Action as a Distinct Concept: Theoretical Foundations of Societal Constitutionalism." In *American Sociological Review* (51): 743–766.

———. Sciulli, D. 1990. "Differentiation and Collegial Formation: Implications of Societal Constitutionalism." In *Differentiation Theory and Social Change*, edited by Alexander J.C., Colomy P., 367–405. New York: Columbia University Press.

Schluchter, W. "The Paradox of Rationalization: On the Relations of Ethics and World." In *Max Weber's Vision of History. Ethics and Methods*, edited by Roth G., Schluchter W., 11–64. Berkeley: University of California Press, 1979.

Scott, J.F. "The Changing Foundations of the Parsonian Action Scheme." In *American Sociological Review* (28, 1963): 719–735.

Smelser, N.J. 2001. "Introduction to the Transaction Edition." In Parsons T. and Shils E.A., *Toward a General Theory of Action*, vii-xix. London: Transaction, 2001 (1953).

———. Smelser, N.J. 2005a. "Parsons' Economic Sociology and the Development of Economic Sociology." In *After Parsons*, edited by Fox R.C., Lidz V.M., and Bershady H.J., 31–43. New York: Russell Sage Foundation.

———. Smelser, N.J. 2005b. "Parsons' Economic Sociology and its Extension to the Global Economy." In *Journal of Classical Sociology* (5): 245–266.

Staubmann, H. "Culture as a Subsystem of Action: Autonomous and Heteronomous Functions." In *After Parsons*, edited by Fox R.C., Lidz V.M., and Bershady H.J., 169–178. New York: Russell Sage Foundation, 2005.

Swedberg, R. "Thematic Issue – Guest Editor's Introduction." In *Sociological Inquiry* (61, 1991): 2–9.

Tiryakian, E.A. 1975. "Neither Marx nor Durkheim... Perhaps Weber." In *American Journal of Sociology* (81): 1–33.

———. Tiryakian, E.A. 1992. "Dialectics of Modernity." In *Social Change and Modernity*, edited by Haferkamp H., Smelser N.J., 78–94. Berkeley: University of California Press.

———. Tiryakian, E.A. 2005. "Parsons and the Human Condition." In *After Parsons*, edited by Fox R.C., Lidz V.M., Bershady H.J., 267–288. New York: Russell Sage.

———.Treviño, J. "Parsons' Action-System Requisite Model and Weber's Elective Affinity: A Convergence of Convenience." In *Journal of Classical Sociology* (5, 2005): 319–348.

Turner, R.J. 1986a. "Sickness and Social Structure: Parsons' Contribution to Medical Sociology." In *Talcott Parsons on Economy and Society*, edited by Holton R.J. and Turner B., 107–142. London: Routledge.

———. Turner, R.J. 1986b. "Parsons and His Critics: on the Ubiquity of Functionalism." In *Talcott Parsons on Economy and Society*, edited by Holton R.J. and Turner B., 179–206. London: Routledge.

———. Turner, R.J. 1998. *The Structure of Sociological Theory*. Belmont, CA: Wadsworth.

Vanderstraeten, R. "Parsons, Luhmann and the Theorem of Double Contingency." In *Journal of Classical Sociology* (2, 2002): 77–92.

Warner, R.S. 1981. "Parsons's Last Testament." In *American Journal of Sociology* (87): 715–721.

———. Warner, R.S. 2006 (1978). "Toward a Redefinition of Action Theory: Paying the Cognitive Element its Due." In *American Journal of Sociology* (83): 1317–1349.

Wenzel, H. 1986. *Einleitung des Herausgebers: Einige Bemerkungen zu Parsons' Program einer Theorie des Handelns.* Frankfurt: Suhrkamp.

———.Wenzel, H. 2005. "Social Order as Communication: Parsons's Theory on the Move from Moral Consensus to Trust." In *After Parsons*, edited by Fox R.C., Lidz V.M., and Bershady H.J., 66–82. New York: Russell Sage Foundation.

White, W. F. "Parsonian Theory Applied to Organizations." In *The Social Theories of Talcott Parsons*, edited by Black M., 250–267. Englewood Cliffs, N.J.: Prentice Hall, 1961.

Williams, R.M. "The Sociological Theory of Talcott Parsons." In *The Social Theories of Talcott Parsons,* edited by Black M., 64–99. Englewood Cliffs, N.J.: Prentice Hall, 1961.

Wrong, D. "The Oversocialized Conception of Man in Modern Sociology." In *The American Sociological Review* (26, 1961): 183–193.

Zaret, D. "From Weber to Parsons and Schutz: The Eclipse of History in Modern Social Theory." In *American Journal of Sociology* (85, 1980): 1180–1201.

Index

academic freedom, 73, 77
action, 1, 13; analytically considered,
2; as subjective, 103; defined, 1; in
second period, 27; in third period,
57; instrumental vs. expressive, 2;
restraints on, 11
action orientation, 5-6, 19
action rationality, 11
action system(s): and organic systems,
52; evolution of, 52; in third period,
37-41
action, theory of: and human situation,
71; inconsistent with voluntarism,
104
Actor, Situation and Normative Pattern,
14, 104
actor, 1-2; orientation to system, 17
adaptation, 6
adaptive function: in second period, 28
adaptive upgrading, 8, 117; and social
change (third period), 37-39
Addario: Parsons' conception of society,
99
affectivity vs. effective neutrality, 19;
dilemma of, 20
African-Americans: as disadvantaged,
65-67; social inclusion of, 58

AGIL pattern/scheme, 26; and
cybernetic hierarchy, 36; and human
condition, 67; and Parson's later
essays, 83; and pattern variable
frame, 26; and research activities,
65; in *Economy and Society*, 34; in
second period, 28; in third period,
37, 41
American Academy of Arts and
Sciences: *Daedelus*, 70; Parsons'
presidency of, 70
American "nuclear" family, 68
American Society, 41, 54-56, 86; AGIL
and human condition, 57
American society: government vs.
private interests, 54
An Outline of the Social System, 26
analytical realism: alternatives to, 100;
principle of, 12
anomy, problem of: and Nazism, 83;
and Protestant religious heritage in
U.S., 97; in post WWI Germany, 60;
risk of in U.S., 97

Bales, 26
Berger: critique of Parsons theory of
social action, 96-97

135

Made in the USA
Middletown, DE
23 May 2016